INSIDE THE
STEALTH BOMBER

BILL SWEETMAN

MBI Publishing Company

This book is respectfully dedicated to the engineers and US Air Force personnel who made the B-2 possible, and to family members who endured long separations for reasons that they were not cleared to know.

• • •

Special thanks to Irv Waaland, John Cashen and Dr. Paul Kaminski, who made themselves available for lengthy interviews; to Jim Goodall, for help with photographs; to Capt. Bruce Sprecher and colleagues at the 509th Bomb Wing; and, as always, to Mary Pat, Martin and Evan for their patience and support.

First published in 1999 by MBI Publishing Company, 729 Prospect Avenue, PO Box 1, Osceola, WI 54020-0001 USA

MBI Publishing Company books are also available at discounts in bulk quantity for industrial or sales-promotional use. For details write to Special Sales Manager at Motorbooks International Wholesalers & Distributors, 729 Prospect Avenue, Osceola, WI 54020-0001 USA.

Library of Congress Cataloging-in-Publication Data Available
ISBN 0-7603-0627-3

On the front cover: *Missouri* (AV-8) at Palmdale, ready for delivery to the 509th. This view shows the rugged construction of the main landing gear doors and even the auxiliary air inlets: apertures on a stealth aircraft must be rigid to prevent them from gapping in flight. The weapon bay doors are open and the spoilers are extended. *Northrop*

On the frontispiece: The blending of low-observable technologies with high aerodynamic efficiency and large payload gives the B-2 important advantages over existing bombers. Its low-observability provides it greater freedom of action at high altitudes, thus increasing its range and a better field of view for the aircraft's sensors. *Nebraska* (AV-13), shown here, first arrived at Whiteman AFB on June 28, 1995. *Northrop*

On the title page: The split brake-rudders, directly borrowed from the XB-35 and YB-49, are highly effective control surfaces. As they approach their full deflection angles, small covers open to let the hinges pass through the skin. This keeps the rudder gaps small during normal cruising flight while allowing them to open wide at low airspeeds. *Northrop*

On the back cover, top: The B-2 weapon system trainer was one of the world's most sophisticated simulators at the time of its introduction. (It was developed by Link, but after a series of mergers, Raytheon now runs the program.) Particularly challenging features included the need to replicate the B-2's radar display and defensive management system, accurately reproducing the way that they would respond to real-world targets and threats. *Northrop*

On the back cover, bottom: The B-2's windshield is huge, but the crew sits well behind it and the view from the cockpit is limited. The B-2 was built with a third crew station, in case the crew workload made it necessary (the dotted outline of the ejection hatch is visible) but this has not been used either in flight test or in operations. The diamond-shaped patch on the leading edge, to the left of the seam in the leading-edge RAM assembly, may cover an antenna for the defensive management system. *Northrop*

Printed in Hong Kong

CONTENTS

INTRODUCTION

In October 1998, Yugoslavia's unlovely president, Slobodan Milosevich, ordered his gallant Serbian forces to comply with NATO demands and cease their activities against ethnic Albanian civilians. Milosevich did not do this out of the goodness of his heart, if such a thing exists, but because he faced the threat of air strikes. Having spent three-quarters of his national treasury on weapons over the past few years, Milosevich was not ready to see that investment destroyed.

The Serbian leader's climb-down came just four days after six B-52 bombers, just short of 40 years old, were deployed to Royal Air Force Fairford in the United Kingdom. Obviously, there were many other forces already in the theater, but the B-52s gave Milosevich a new set of problems to worry about. Maybe they carried long-range cruise missiles, which could destroy fixed targets anywhere in his territory without exposing a single American to any Yugoslavian weapon. On the other hand, the Americans might have finally had it up to their ears with Milosevich and decided that his record made him a poor choice as a martyr: for all Milosevich knew, special forces might be tracking his movements and the B-52s might be armed with AGM-142 missiles, capable of hitting a single door or window from 70 miles away in the middle of the night. If all pretense at subtlety was to be abandoned, the B-52s could pound Serbian weapon and ammunition dumps with tons of ordnance, obliterating them in a blaze of secondary explosions as they did in Desert Storm.

Despite its amazing career and extraordinary flexibility, the B-52 is in the twilight of its service life. It requires a lot of maintenance and support, but its chief limitation is its vulnerability to air defenses. Except as a long-range cruise-missile launcher, the B-52 cannot be launched unless other aircraft have taken the enemy's surface-to-air missiles and fighters out of the picture.

Rewind the news tape to late 1990, as the West confronts Saddam Hussein's Iraq. The deadline for Iraqi forces to leave Kuwait is days away. Western news organizations have hired colonels and generals as military analysts, and their conclusions are gloomy. Iraq's Soviet-supplied integrated air defense system (IADS) will prevent the coalition's air forces from achieving a clear victory in the air, they say. An air campaign will incur heavy losses of men and machines, but will not avert a bloody combined arms battle on the ground.

The media analysts were dramatically wrong. The IADS was blinded and lobotomized in the first minutes of the air campaign and never recovered. Thereafter, the coalition knew more about what was going on in the skies above Iraq than the Iraqis themselves. The West's ability to do this hinged on its use of a weapon that could simultaneously defeat both missiles and concrete, avoiding SAMs while delivering penetrating bombs to destroy bunkers that cruise missiles could barely scratch. This was the F-117 stealth fighter.

The F-117 was a technological breakthrough, but its design was compromised in favor of getting the aircraft into service quickly. The F-117s in the Gulf required extensive tanker support and were limited to clear-night attacks on presurveyed, fixed targets.

One aircraft in the world, however, combines the B-52's range, autonomy, and lethality with the survivability of the F-117: the Northrop Grumman B-2. You might think that it would be regarded as a unique, vital national asset. Instead, it has been mismanaged and vilified to the point where most people regard it as a massively expensive failure. Congress, which is largely responsible for much of the cost of the project, and almost wholly responsible for cutting the number built to a bare minimum, has refused to revisit the need for the aircraft. The U.S. Air Force and the aircraft's designers have been encouraged to refrain from overzealous lobbying on its behalf, restrained by rigid security rules.

The B-2 has never been perfect, but history will record that its biggest defect was its timing. It was conceived at the crux of the Cold War. It was a time when many military professionals believed that the clock was close to midnight, and that instability within the Soviet Union, combined with its military strength, could lead to a desperate all-out war. But as the program entered its most difficult phase, and as tests revealed unexpected problems (and it is always hard to persuade the denizens of Capitol Hill, where lawyers vastly outnumber engineers, that the purpose of a test is to find problems), the Cold War came to an abrupt and quite unexpected end.

The B-2 became a symbol, not a weapon. It symbolized the defense build-up of the 1980s and all its allegedly profligate spending. By attacking the B-2, the Democrat-controlled Congress could attack the Reagan and Bush administrations, which their party had failed to beat at the ballot box. They could show themselves fiscally responsible, even though they did not have the stomach to cancel the program outright, and instead squandered billions of dollars by delaying its progress and slowing production to a crawl.

Unfortunately, there was no effective public debate over the B-2. The decisions that doomed the program were made in 1989–1991, when most details of the aircraft were shrouded in secrecy. Outside the armed forces and the contractor team, the only people with access to information were members of congressional committees who had already decided to maim the program. Every problem was publicized, the solutions were implemented in secret, and the bomber's potential was never discussed.

There are two lessons to be learned from this story. One is that there is a drawback to the legislative branch's control of large military programs: the taxpayers foot the bill for congressional micromanagement long after those responsible have moved on to other offices. The other is that secrecy can protect a new technology from hostile countermeasures, but what use is that when it helps domestic adversaries ensure that the technology never reaches the troops?

THE TALE OF THE WHALE

December 17, 1993, would have been cold in southern Missouri even if you were not standing in the middle of a windswept airfield, under a ragged and spattering sky. Kansas City, with its blues, barbecue, and indoor heating, seemed a long way off to those waiting on that field.

That was when the B-2 arrived, dropping through a rent in the clouds. Those who never had seen a B-2 in the air before forgot how cold they were, because a B-2 in flight is a strange and mystifying sight that changes from second to second. Head-on, it is barely visible at the other end of the airfield, a charcoal-pencil stroke across your vision. From the side, a flying saucer from a 1950s movie, its wings invisible. Overhead, a manta-ray executed in black by Picasso.

The bomber landed, the first of its type to join the 509th Bomb Wing at Whiteman Air Force Base, Missouri, close to the bustling metropolis of Knob Noster. It was handed over in a brief ceremony. Defense Secretary Les Aspin, who had just tendered his resignation, was not present. Air Force Secretary Sheila Widnall was, but she answered few questions. The date at which the B-2 would become operational was still classified. Somehow, a gray cloud seemed to surround the B-2, even when the sun was shining.

Now, as the bomber finally nears full operational capability with the 509th, more of its extraordinary story can be put together. It is a tale of determination and innovation that defies most comparisons. It's enough to say that the Manhattan Project, the development of the U.S. Navy's Fleet Ballistic Missile program, and the B-2 can probably be mentioned in the same breath, and to remind the reader that Leonardo da Vinci, had you asked him his occupation, would probably have answered, "Military engineer."

The Whale's wide cockpit accommodated a single pilot. The dorsal air intake for the two Garrett AiResearch ATF3 engines was entirely flush with the upper fuselage, which was good from the RCS viewpoint but bad for pressure recovery. The flared ends of the V-tails were considered necessary for low RCS, although the later YF-23 had straight surfaces. *Bill Sweetman*

This poor-quality image is the only unclassified picture to show the full-scale radar cross-section (RCS) model of Northrop's Have Blue design. With a diamond-shaped planform and a top-mounted inlet, the Northrop design could not match the all-aspect low RCS of its Lockheed rival. *Northrop*

The technology that made the B-2 possible originated in the mid-1970s from two unrelated developments. After the successful use of remotely piloted vehicles (RPVs) in Vietnam, the U.S. Air Force and industry researchers looked at smaller, less complex mini-RPVs. In the process, a Teledyne Ryan mini-RPV was flown against both U.S. and foreign radars at Eglin Air Force Base, Florida, and proved very difficult to detect.

Meanwhile, the Pentagon's scientific consulting group, the Defense Science Board, completed its annual Summer Study for 1974. With fresh experience in Vietnam and the 1973 air battles over the Middle East, the Defense Science Board concluded that conventional aircraft would face severe challenges surviving against the type of robust, networked air defense system the Soviet Union was developing.

In the early fall, the Pentagon's deputy director for research and engineering, Malcolm Currie, brought a request to a group at Wright-Patterson Air Force Base in Dayton, Ohio, which supported the Defense Advanced Research Projects Agency (DARPA) and had links to the U.S. Air Force scientists who had been researching the subject of radar cross-section (RCS) for decades: could they build a manned aircraft with a signature as low as the tiny mini-RPV?

Despite a great deal of work on RCS reduction in the 1950s and 1960s—including the testing and operational use of stealthy drones and reconnaissance aircraft and the use of RCS-reduction technology on the Hound Dog missile—the smallest RCS achieved for a real aircraft was still too large for the aircraft to survive by stealth alone. On the Hound Dog, stealth bought time as the missile bored in on the SAM sites it was intended to destroy. On the Teledyne Ryan AQM-91 Firefly drone, it was combined with high altitude, and on the SR-71 it was combined with altitude and speed.

Late in 1974, DARPA contacted the main U.S. manufacturers of fighters and other military aircraft to determine which of them might be interested in bidding on the Stealth study. It was a low-profile project, but not particularly secret, because nobody knew whether or not it would even be important. In January 1975, DARPA awarded small contracts to McDonnell Douglas and Northrop, calling for designs for a low-RCS manned aircraft. Neither weapons nor sensors need be carried, and at this stage there was no guarantee that there would be money to take the project further.

At Northrop's Aircraft Division, the DARPA proposal arrived two months after John Cashen joined the division. Cashen had been a phenomenologist at Hughes, tasked with defining what targets looked like to the company's radar and infrared sensors. He joined Northrop in 1973 to work on lasers.

Cashen gathered a solid background in signatures through his work at Hughes, including the work done on the Boeing Short-Range Attack Missile and other missiles. A forceful personality, not reticent about putting his views forward, Cashen became the leader and spokesman for the more junior electromagnet-

Eleven years after the single Northrop Tacit Blue prototype made its last test flight, the U.S. Air Force officially disclosed the existence of the long-rumored "Shamu." It turned out that it was other companies' engineers who had given it that name; to its builders, it was simply known as "the Whale." The nickname became so sensitive that one of the designers advised his wife not to wear a pin in the shape of a whale that she had bought in Maine, to her great puzzlement. *Bill Sweetman*

"I didn't know Airstream built airplanes," was one of the many jokes leveled at the Whale. Behind the cockpit, the largest element of the long forward fuselage was an open-sided bay for the Hughes battlefield surveillance radar. It had a two-sided array, with a radar on one side and a datalink on the other, and it could rotate around the airplane's long axis to point the radar left or right. *Bill Sweetman*

ics experts on the team. "I was well aware that RCS was not dependent on size, area, or volume," he says. RCS "is local. If you deal with each local phenomenon, you can make a very large object very small on radar."

Headed by Cashen, and using the RCS-prediction equations that had been developed at universities in the 1950s and 1960s, the Northrop group started to work on the DARPA requirement. They were joined by Irv Waaland, a veteran hands-on designer who came to Northrop from Grumman barely a year earlier. The work started with "a lot of systems analysis," Waaland recalls. "While the RCS people were estimating how low they could get, we did systems analysis to deter-

mine what kind of reductions would be required to impact the air defenses."

Northrop's goal was to develop a low-altitude attack aircraft, and the analysts concluded that it was most important to reduce its RCS from the nose and tail. Detecting a low-flying airplane from the side is difficult, because look-down radars rely on the Doppler effect caused by the target's movement relative to the radar and to the ground beneath it. Because it is less easy to shoot down an airplane in a tail-chase, the tail-on signature was less important than the nose.

It has often been stated that Northrop's approach to stealth relied on advancing computer technology, but Cashen tells a different story. "If we'd had a computer [that could predict RCS] we'd have used it," he says. "We were not able to synthesize RCS; we couldn't get a complete answer. It was better to use experience and the tools that we had and do it experimentally. We ended up using a shaping solution that, in general, ended up working when we tested it."

Lockheed's Skunk Works was not asked to compete in the project, but found out about the project and entered the fray using its own funds. Lockheed and Northrop both outperformed their competition, and in September 1975 they were awarded contracts to design a stealth demonstrator, known as the Experimental Survivable Testbed, or XST. Each company would build a full-scale RCS model for a "pole-off" at the U.S. Air Force's RCS range at Holloman Air Force Base in New Mexico.

Northrop had two problems: first, the Northrop XST was designed on the assumption that the nose-on RCS was more important than the rear aspect. Its plan-view shape was a diamond with more sweep on the leading edges than the trailing edges. From the rear, it sustained its low RCS as long as the radar was no more than 35 degrees off the tail, but beyond that the radar would be at right angles to the trailing edge.

Unfortunately, the DARPA requirement treated RCS by quadrants: The rear quadrant extended to 45 degrees either side of the tail, taking in the Northrop design's RCS spikes. Waaland could not solve the problem by stretching the tail and increasing the sweep angle because the diamond-shaped aircraft would become uncontrollable. Lockheed, however, had made the jump to a swept-wing aircraft with a deeply notched trailing edge and could handle the problem.

Tacit Blue program manager Steve Smith, center, with two of the men who played key roles on the B-2. Irv Waaland (left) brought a long background in engineering to the program. John Cashen (right) headed the electromagnetics group. The two disciplines were often in competition: "You know just enough to be dangerous," was Cashen's retort when Waaland challenged him on a design issue. *Bill Sweetman*

Northrop's other shortcoming was radar absorbent material (RAM). Northrop was unaware of Lockheed's long background of work on RAM, including the sophisticated high-temperature plastic used in the SR-71's leading edges. In June 1975, the Air Force convened a secret radar camouflage symposium at Wright-Patterson, where the Skunk Works' Kelly Johnson revealed the decade-old-secret of the SR-71's stealth technology, but it was too late to catch up in time to compete in XST.

Lockheed also proved bolder in designing its XST and more willing to abandon design conventions to ensure that its design would be extremely stealthy. Northrop's design had curved wing surfaces. Lockheed built its entire shape from flat plates. Northrop used a top-mounted inlet with a serpentine duct and a mesh screen; Lockheed adopted inlet grills. There was disappointment but little surprise when Lockheed was selected to build XST in March 1976, under the code name Have Blue.

DARPA and the Air Force wanted a second source of stealth technology, but preferred not to focus attention on the secret magic of stealth by holding another open competition. In December 1976, DARPA approached Northrop about an agency project called Assault Breaker. Its goal was to stop a Soviet tank attack in Central Europe with precision-guided weapons. It depended on an airborne radar to track the tanks and the incoming missiles—but how would a radar-carrying airplane survive within line-of-sight of its targets?

The answer was what DARPA called Battlefield Surveillance Aircraft-Experimental (BSAX). DARPA planned to award this program to Northrop, both to keep Northrop's stealth technology moving and to avoid the risk of distracting Lockheed from Have Blue.

BSAX was considerably more difficult than Have Blue. A stealth aircraft has been described as a very inefficient antenna that flies, but a radar antenna has to be an efficient reflector. The radar-range equation was also at work: a radar signal that is strong enough to detect a target can itself be intercepted at a much greater distance.

While Have Blue was an attack aircraft, intended to make a straight run for its target and to spend as little time in a defended area as possible, BSAX would have to loiter over the battlefield for hours, during which it would be illuminated by many radars from different directions. Unlike Have Blue, which was more detectable from the side than from the front and rear, BSAX would have to be the first "all-aspect stealth" design.

Part of the solution was in hand at Hughes, which was already working on low probability of intercept (LPI) technology (the radar world's equivalent of stealth) and designing low-RCS antennas.

As Northrop started to design BSAX, the Ford administration packed its bags in Washington. The incoming Carter team, including Defense Secretary Harold Brown and Dr. William Perry, deputy secretary of defense for research and development, was heavy with engineers and academics. Perry himself had built up his own company to manufacture electronics for the Pentagon and intelligence agencies.

One of Perry's first actions on stealth was to appoint Air Force scientist Paul Kaminski "to serve as his technical conscience," as Kaminski puts it. "Was it real or not?" Kaminski's report was positive. The next step was more difficult. Assuming that Have Blue worked, how should stealth be used?

Some high-level discussions followed in the spring of 1977, involving Perry, General Al Slay, chief of Air Force research and development, and General Robert Bond, a rising Air Force star who later died while flying a MiG at Area 51. The support group included two majors, Ken Staton and Joe Ralston (in late 1998, the latter was vice-chairman of the Joint Chiefs of Staff).

At a conference in 1990, Ralston remarked that one option studied by the group was whether Stealth research should be shut down, the programs stopped, and the data locked away, because the potential of stealth was so explosive. Stealth did not discriminate between U.S. and Soviet radars, and in the 1970s the Soviet Union was showing a disconcerting tendency to develop new generations of weapons

Apart from the Tacit Blue and B-2, the only known aircraft to use Northrop's stealth shaping technology was the YF-23 Advanced Tactical Fighter candidate, which competed unsuccessfully with the Lockheed YF-22. Two YF-23 prototypes were flown in 1990. *Northrop*

15

on a shorter cycle than the United States. This meant the Soviets could field them more quickly once developed. But Perry, as Kaminski recalls, "thought it was better to run fast than to behave like an ostrich."

The study group looked at how stealth could be applied to any type of conflict, ranging from counter-insurgency operations through regional and European conventional conflict to nuclear deterrence. Large-scale conventional warfare and nuclear attack were seen as the missions where stealth provided the greatest military advantage.

Next, the Pentagon group examined what kind of operational stealth aircraft could and should be developed. The debate closed in on two concepts. The "A airplane" was a scaled-up Have Blue, with the fewest possible changes to its shape, and off-the-shelf systems. It was designed to be fielded quickly with minimum risk and to be deployed as a "silver bullet" system for attacks on a few crucial targets.

The "B airplane" was much larger. Originally, it was designed to carry a 10,000-pound payload on a 1,000-nm-radius mission, but the resulting aircraft proved large and inefficient. Lockheed designers believed they could improve its aerodynamics by using curved wing surfaces, but this would introduce more risk into the design, and it was ruled out. Consequently, even with a 7,500-pound weapon load, the two-crew aircraft would be around the size of the 45-ton FB-111 bomber. Wind tunnel tests of both designs were carried out at NASA's Ames Research Center in 1978.

There was some enthusiasm for the larger aircraft within the Air Force, particularly after the new administration canceled the B-1 in June 1977. The Strategic Air Command was particularly supportive of the larger aircraft,

but the small LO (low observable) group within the Pentagon felt that it was risky. "We had much less confidence that we could pull that design off," says Ralston. "There were some tough decisions that had to be made by a small group of people." One critical issue was whether or not a single pilot could perform the mission envisaged for the smaller aircraft. "We flew a simulator and found one person could do it."

In the summer of 1978, the Air Force decided to focus on the A design. This was the Advanced Tactical Aircraft (ATA), later designated F-117A. The service continued to fund Lockheed's studies of the larger bomber, however. Because the B-1 had been canceled and the immediate need to field a stealth aircraft was met by the ATA, the bomber design became more influenced by SAC's needs, and it grew in size and performance.

These decisions had little immediate impact on Northrop, which was preoccupied with BSAX. The design matured as an awkward-looking aircraft designed rather like a Huey helicopter around a huge box with open sides. The concept was to concentrate all the radar reflectivity into one "spike" at right angles to the body and to maneuver the aircraft so that the spikes never dwelt on a hostile radar.

Northrop put the first BSAX models on the pole in the summer of 1977. "It was a disaster," says Waaland, who was summoned to rescue the program. DARPA's Ken Perko, worried that Northrop might not be able to make BSAX work, quietly invited Lockheed to study the concept.

It was Fred Oshira, one of Cashen's electromagneticists, who saved Northrop's face. With the BSAX problems constantly in his mind, Oshira took to carrying a piece of modeling clay at all times, even when he took his family to Disneyland. Sitting on a bench, watching his children on the teacup ride, Oshira molded the clay into a new shape, with a rounded top and flat sloped sides that flared down and outward into a knife-edge.

It worked like a charm, flowing the radar energy around the body rather than scattering it like a mirror. Northrop had not only found a way to remain stealthy from any direction, but had significantly expanded the range of radar frequencies that stealth technology could defeat. Northrop's philosophy was also inherently compatible with curvature, promising greater aerodynamic efficiency.

Again, better computers helped, "but we didn't design the aircraft on the computer," says Waaland. "Computers allowed us to look at parts of the aircraft in two dimensions. We could blend them together, but we didn't have an integrated model."

With the major RCS problem solved, the BSAX design came together in the second half of 1977. It had a bluff-nosed, bulky body to accommodate the radar. The engines were buried at the rear behind a flush dorsal inlet, with no screens or grilles. It had an unswept wing, which used a Clark Y airfoil section that had not been seen since the 1930s. The advantage was that the lower surface was flat. Pitch and yaw were controlled by a fly-by-wire system driving two all-moving V-tails. Worried about how the ends of the angled tail would appear on radar, the designers curved the tips of the V-tails toward the horizon. It was a final, organic touch to the design, which soon acquired the nickname "Whale." DARPA awarded the company a contract for a single prototype in April 1978.

By the end of that year, there were several stealth programs under development. Have Blue was flying. Its operational derivative, the F-117, was the subject of a development contract late in 1978. Lockheed was working on the still-classified Senior Prom air-launched cruise missile—and a stealthy nuclear bomber.

CHAPTER TWO

A BOMBER? FROM NORTHROP?

Even though the Carter administration had canceled the B-1 only months before, it was increasingly committed, in secrecy, to developing a new bomber. U.S. nuclear deterrence relied on a "triad" of systems— bombers, ICBMs, and submarine-launched missiles—which supported one another, because it was impossible for an adversary to attack them all at the same time.

In the late 1970s, however, CIA analysis showed an emerging "window of vulnerability." In a first strike, more accurate Soviet ICBMs would destroy more U.S. ICBMs on the ground. This would mean that the bombers would be attacking an almost intact and fully operational Soviet air-defense system, and this system itself was being strengthened. Cities and other targets were being ringed with high-power radars and new missiles. The new long-range MiG-31 interceptor was designed to push the air battle hundreds of miles farther from the targets, over the Arctic, so that the vulnerable B-52s could be engaged before they were within cruise-missile range of their objectives.

By 1979, the Carter administration had secretly authorized the start of a stealth bomber program. The requirement became more demanding, and the Lockheed design evolved to meet it. It acquired curvature on the wings and rounded edges rather than sharply defined facets, although its surfaces were curved in one dimension rather than two and the shape still retained flat surfaces. But, as the Air Force continued to refine its requirement, the Pentagon's planners began to question whether this would be enough.

The requirement came to be based on the assumption that the bombers would have to penetrate for hundreds of miles into Soviet territory after a successful first strike by Soviet missiles had destroyed the U.S. ICBM force.

Flown in June 1946, the XB-35 was one of the most awesome sights in aviation history. Not only was it devoid of any separate control surfaces, but it was one of the largest aircraft of its day. The flight test program was plagued by problems with the contra-rotating propellers, but the principal problem was that its multiple bomb bays were designed for high-explosive World War II ordnance and could not accommodate the bulky nuclear weapons of the 1940s. *Northrop*

1970s Boeing study with V-tails. Lacking the theoretical background in LO design that Lockheed and Northrop had developed, and limited to small-scale RCS testing, Boeing could not develop comparably stealthy designs. After 1980, however, manufacturers were told not to discuss stealth technology outside classified forums. *Boeing*

This meant that they would have fully operational threat radars all around them: hence, the requirement for a very low RCS in all bandwidths and from all directions. Northrop's all-aspect, wide-bandwidth stealth technology began to look very promising.

The Air Force also wanted the ability to determine if targets had already been attacked and to threaten the mobile missile launchers that the Soviet Union was developing, so the bomber would need a "stealthy" radar with long range and high resolution—exactly what Hughes and Northrop had been developing in the Tacit Blue program.

Northrop was not known as a builder of large aircraft, and its last bomber program (the B-35/B-49 flying wing) had almost destroyed it, so it took some high-level persuasion from the Air Force before the company would even begin a small-scale bomber study.

Northrop's analysis found a weakness in the Soviet air defenses: Although they were being bolstered against low-level penetrators and cruise missiles, they remained thinner at high altitudes. The designers concluded that they needed a bomber capable of U-2-like altitudes, with a planform shape that generated the smallest possible number of RCS "spikes." High altitude meant a large wing area and span.

In the summer of 1979, designer Hal Markarian produced a sketch that is a recognizable ancestor of the B-2, in the arrangement of its basic components and the philosophy that drove them. It was also quite unlike anything that had gone before it.

The only aircraft that had ever looked remotely like the Northrop design were flown in the 1940s, when designers in the United States, Britain, and Germany were pursuing the idea

This Boeing study for a low-altitude stealth bomber dates back to 1979 when it was publicly released. Boeing could do this because the company was entirely unaware that a full-scale stealth bomber was already underway. *Boeing*

of an all-wing aircraft or flying wing. As its name suggests, the all-wing aircraft has neither fuselage nor tail, but carries all its payload, fuel, and components inside the wing. But even those distant ancestors did not share the single dominating, most bizarre feature of the shape that Markarian designed.

Viewed from directly above or below, the boomerang-like shape comprised eight ruler-straight lines. The leading edges, the long sides of the boomerang, ran straight from the extreme

In 1981, the new Reagan administration was faced with two candidates to replace the B-52: the promising, but very risky stealth bomber and an improved version of the Rockwell B-1. Four prototypes of the swing-wing B-1 had already been built and had logged almost 1,900 hours. This persuaded the Pentagon to order 100 B-1Bs and to defer deliveries of an operational stealth bomber into the early 1990s. *Rockwell*

nose to the extreme tips of the wing. The wingtips were not parallel with the airflow, like those on most normal aircraft, but were cut off at a near-right-angle to the leading edges. Apart from the tips, the outer wings had no taper. Again, this was completely unlike any normal aircraft. The inner trailing edges kinked sharply and jutted rearward toward the centerline. A closer inspection would show that the edges formed two groups of four exactly parallel lines.

Each feature was determined by a different subset of the mission requirements. It was a flying wing, because there is nothing quite as stealthy as a flat plate viewed edge-on, and the flying wing was the closest practical approach to such a shape. Also, it was clear from the first empirical stealth studies that a highly blended shape, with minimal tail surfaces, was a good starting point for a stealth design. A blended shape provided more space for internal weapons and buried engines.

A distant precursor of the B-2 design was the Horten Ho IX flying-wing jet bomber of 1944. A production version was to have been skinned with a radar-absorbent sandwich material, comprising a mixture of sawdust, carbon, and glue between plywood layers. The first Ho IX, the only aircraft of the type to fly, crashed in 1945, but the third prototype survives in the Smithsonian collection. *via Motor-Buch Verlag*

Flying wings and their advocates—including Jack Northrop, the company's founder, and the Horten brothers, Walter and Reimar—have existed as long as the aircraft itself. The flying wing, these advocates argued, will carry the same payload as far as a conventional aircraft while weighing less and using less fuel. The weight and drag of the tail surfaces are absent, as is the weight of the structure that supports them. The wing structure itself is more efficient, because the weight of the aircraft is spread across the wing rather than being concentrated in the center. Northrop's XB-35 was designed to equal the bomb load and range of the Convair B-36, but with two-thirds the gross weight and power.

There are long-standing arguments against the flying wing too. The modern large jet has a relatively small, highly loaded wing that is the right size for climb and cruise. Takeoff and landing speeds are reduced with the help of flaps, and the trim change caused by the flaps is canceled out by the tail. The flying wing has no tail, and hence no flaps, so its wing must be larger, and, by conventional standards, oversized. But Northrop had already determined that a higher cruising altitude was an operational benefit for the new bomber, so the large wing was a positive advantage. The new bomber would cruise at 70,000 feet, almost as high as the U-2 spy plane.

The requirement sized and shaped the aircraft. Payload and range set a lower limit to the wingspan. The leading-edge sweep angle was determined by the desired high-subsonic cruising speed and by the need to locate the aerodynamic center close to the center of gravity. Given that the wing extends to the front of the vehicle, it must be swept back to place the center of lift where it needs to be.

Winning the ATB competition was a replay of the most dramatic—and traumatic—era in Northrop's history. In late 1941, Northrop won a contract for the XB-35 intercontinental-range flying-wing bomber, promising to match the range and bomb load of the more conventional B-36 on two-thirds as much power. A subscale version of the bomber, the N-9M, was tested to explore stability and control issues. *Northrop*

Jack Northrop in front of the YB-49, the jet-powered development of the XB-35. A fervent advocate of the flying wing, Northrop left the industry after the Air Force canceled the project. No larger all-wing aircraft would fly until 1989. *Northrop*

The length of the center-body section was determined by depth: It had to be deep enough to accommodate a cockpit and the weapon bays, and this meant that it had to be a minimum length to avoid excessive drag at high subsonic speeds. Outboard of the center-body section, the chord was set by the need to integrate the engines and their low-observable inlet and exhaust systems into the wing. The inlets and exhaust were set well aft and well forward of the wing edges, the better to shield them from radar.

Details of the shape reflected Northrop's low-RCS design philosophy. Developed and tested on Tacit Blue, it was quite straightforward but resulted in very unusual-looking aircraft because it rested on two fundamental principles that influenced different parts of the aircraft in completely different ways.

The RCS of a conventional aircraft, which is a random irregular shape from an electromagnetic viewpoint, varies sharply with the aspect angle; that is, the radar's bearing from the aircraft. Whenever a radar illuminates the aircraft, most of its energy bounces off the surface like light from a mirror. The energy may be reflected again from another part of the aircraft (bouncing off the body to the wing, for example). Some of the energy will creep along the skin like St. Elmo's fire, and these surface currents will be scattered whenever it reaches a gap or a change in conductivity.

A basic principle behind low-RCS design is that a flat plate has both the largest and smallest RCS of any simple shape. If the plate is normal to the radar beam, its RCS is enormous; but if it is rotated away from the beam in one dimension, its RCS is far smaller, and if it is rotated in two dimensions (rotated and canted) its RCS is infinitesimal.

In the F-117, Lockheed's designers produced a shape composed entirely of flat plates, aligned so that they were, at almost all times, angled away from the radar beam in two dimensions. What makes this possible is the fact that the radar sources that are tactically significant are located in a narrow band of elevations around the aircraft. This led to a secondary problem, however: the sharp edges scattered the surface currents. Unable to model these effects fully, Lockheed smothered them into insignificance by "candy-coating" the entire aircraft with RAM.

Cashen's electromagneticists saw that the same results—ensuring that every part of the surface was angled away from the radar in two dimensions—could also be achieved if the surface was curved. Indeed, if the entire skin of the aircraft comprised one surface, with curving contours of constantly changing radius and direction, there would be no edges or creases at all, avoiding any "hot-spots" in the RCS. This

The eight-jet YB-49 was a spectacular machine, but was not a stable bombing platform without the aid of a stability augmentation system that the Air Force would not trust. Also, despite its jet propulsion, it retained the thick wing of the XB-35 and could not match the speed of Boeing's contemporary B-47. *Northrop*

was the first basic principle of Tacit Blue's shape and was applied to the new bomber.

The second element of the bomber's configuration was common to the F-117. While most of the surfaces could be concealed by radar by making them sloped or curved, the upper and lower surfaces of the aircraft would have to meet at some point. Wing and tail surfaces would also have distinct edges. How should this "waterline" around the aircraft be handled?

The edges and body sides could be treated with RAM, but not well enough to match the low reflectivity of the surfaces. Instead, the designers on both Have Blue teams realized that while the residual reflection from the edges could not be eliminated, it could be controlled, exploiting the fact that the strongest reflection was at right angles to the edge. The design was laid out so that all the edges were grouped along a small number of alignments. The RCS would peak when the radar was normal to one of these edges, but this would happen only transiently, as the aircraft moved relative to the radar and its bearing changed.

Since there is scattering both from the edge of the aircraft that faces the radar and from the edge that faces away from it, the smallest practical number of spikes is four. This can be produced from a pure diamond shape or, since a diamond will not fly very well, from a shape in which all edges conform to two alignments. Markarian took this into account in the design of an eight-sided shape for the B-2.

In a later refinement, both Lockheed and Northrop designers realized that the problem of combining stealth with doors and other apertures could be eased if they conformed to the same alignments as the wing and body edges. If

necessary, door edges could be serrated so that the edges were angled while the aperture itself was roughly rectangular.

The breakthrough that got Northrop out of trouble on Tacit Blue in 1977 was the shaping technique that combined the sharp edges with the curved surfaces: a gradual flare to the knife-edge, still very visible on the lower surfaces of the B-2, combined with continuous curvature to make the energy flow around the aircraft. It is this combination of smoothly curved, seamless surfaces with jagged edges that makes the bomber's appearance so distinctive.

In August 1979, Northrop presented Perry with two designs: Markarian's flying-wing design with parallel edges, using the shaping techniques developed on Tacit Blue, and a diamond-shaped aircraft similar to its Have Blue concept. Perry asked for a further study to flesh out the flying wing design. The maximum cost was $2 million, because a $2 million project did not have to be reported to Congress.

The team was joined by Dick Scherrer, who joined Northrop from Lockheed. Scherrer, Waaland, and aerodynamicist Hans Grellmann started to work out the design details. They developed a $14 million, 11-month proposal (with a $2 million contract price), including wind-tunnel and RCS tests, and Northrop received a contract for the Advanced Strategic Penetration Aircraft (ASPA) in January 1980. "There was one condition," Waaland recalls. "We were advised at the highest levels that we were an insurance policy. We were told not to start lobbying."

A steady stream of visitors from Wright-Patterson, the Strategic Air Command (SAC) and the Pentagon passed through Northrop's offices. Northrop learned from them that the

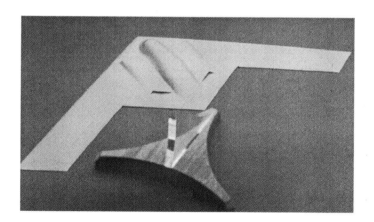

The B-2 takes shape, showing a number of ways of providing directional control. Inward-canted vertical fins were ineffective. After experimenting with tip-mounted fins and reaction jet controls, Northrop settled on a design using split brake-rudders and differential thrust. *Northrop*

As Dr. Paul Kaminski's "Red Team" cautioned that low-altitude penetration might be necessary to defeat large, high-powered radars over the B-2's service life, Northrop assessed the B-2 design to determine the best combination of sweep and wing loading. As shown here, the trade closed at a moderate sweep angle and aspect ratio. *Northrop*

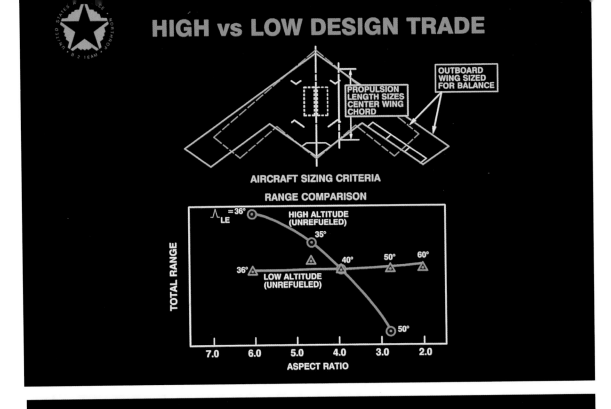

The original B-2 design was built up around a number of key dimensions, to provide space for the crew, weapons bays, and engines in a neutrally stable, efficient package. Note that all the elevons are on the outer wing. *Northrop*

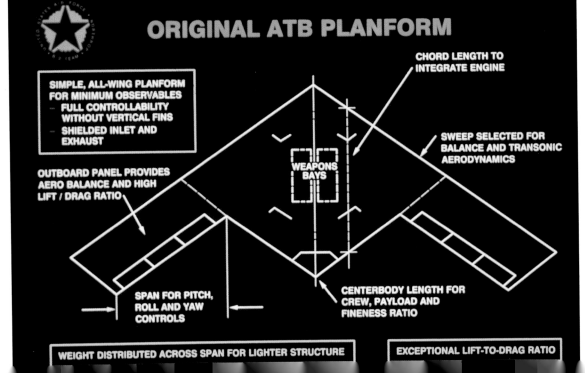

B-2 PLANFORM MODIFICATION

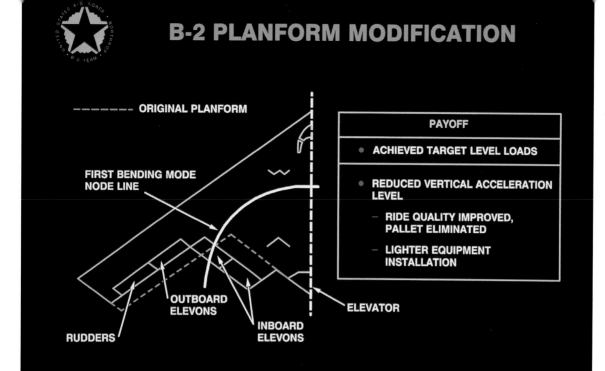

- ---- ORIGINAL PLANFORM

FIRST BENDING MODE NODE LINE

PAYOFF
• ACHIEVED TARGET LEVEL LOADS
• REDUCED VERTICAL ACCELERATION LEVEL
– RIDE QUALITY IMPROVED, PALLET ELIMINATED
– LIGHTER EQUIPMENT INSTALLATION

OUTBOARD ELEVONS

ELEVATOR

INBOARD ELEVONS

RUDDERS

The B-2 was redesigned in 1983 to allow it to fly faster at low level. Because the elevons act to counter the effects of air turbulence, it was necessary to add inboard elevons at a stiffer part of the wing. At the same time, that part of the trailing edge was extended aft to give the new elevons enough leverage, creating the B-2's jagged trailing edge. Finally, the outer wings were made more slender to offset the increased drag of the added wing area inboard. *Northrop*

CONFIGURATION EVOLUTION

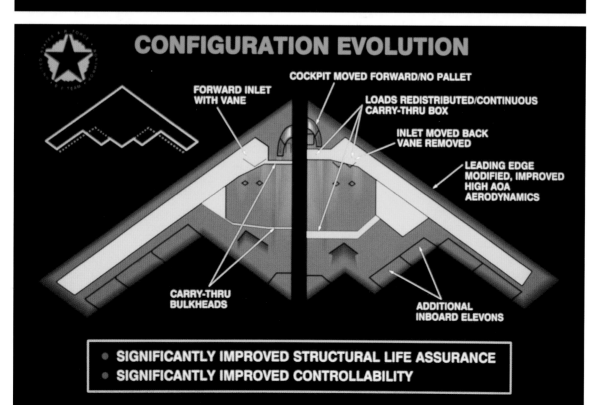

FORWARD INLET WITH VANE

COCKPIT MOVED FORWARD/NO PALLET

LOADS REDISTRIBUTED/CONTINUOUS CARRY-THRU BOX

INLET MOVED BACK VANE REMOVED

LEADING EDGE MODIFIED, IMPROVED HIGH AOA AERODYNAMICS

CARRY-THRU BULKHEADS

ADDITIONAL INBOARD ELEVONS

- • SIGNIFICANTLY IMPROVED STRUCTURAL LIFE ASSURANCE
- • SIGNIFICANTLY IMPROVED CONTROLLABILITY

With the new wing design (right) Northrop also changed the internal structure so that much more of the load would be borne by two massive spars or "carry-through boxes" fore and aft of the weapons bay. The cockpit was moved forward and the inlets aft, to clear the internal structure. The change relieved the loads on the bomber's composite skin, which is nonetheless 1 inch thick in some parts of the center-section. Despite the complete redesign, the schedule was not slipped. *Northrop*

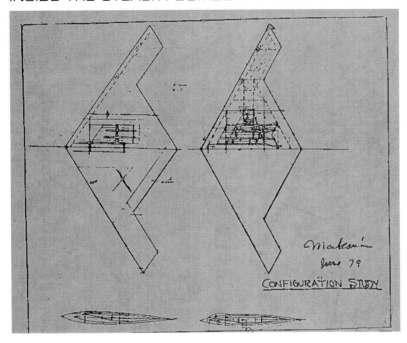

Hal Markarian's initial design for a bomber, dated June 1979, was not unlike the B-2 in planform area but was much lighter and thinner in section, with a small weapons bay and six engines (probably GE F404s). Operating altitude would have been as high as a U-2. *Northrop*

Defense Science Board, commissioned by Perry and Kaminski, had criticized the draft requirement on the grounds that it was too narrow. The Air Force and SAC responded by looking for more weapons capacity and more flexibility. Northrop subtly changed its design, making the bomber's center-section deeper, increasing its weight, and reducing its U-2-like cruising altitude.

As it did so, more details fell into place. Angular in planform, the shape presented only curves from any viewpoint in the horizontal plane. The top and bottom surfaces were both continuous, three-dimensional curved surfaces. Even the overwing air inlets, which looked jagged from a distance, could be seen at close range to be made up of many curved segments. There were even very few curves of constant radius; rather, the surfaces changed radius continuously, as though they were produced from segments of a spiral. The shape had no abrupt distinctions between body and wing; a dorsal hump with the cockpit in front rose smoothly from the top surface, but the underside swelled gradually from the trailing-edge kink to the centerline.

When the U.S. Air Force issued a request for proposals for development and production of the Advanced Technology Bomber (ATB) in September 1980, there was little doubt that Northrop had advanced from an insurance policy to at least equal standing. Lockheed had already teamed with Rockwell for the bomber competition, and Northrop's leaders realized that they would have to find a partner as well. Jones asked for a meeting with Boeing's chairman, Thornton T. Wilson. With one company chief on either side of a long table, flanked by their subordinates, Jones told Wilson about the ATB competition and invited Boeing to join Northrop. It was one of the most valuable contests in history, but Wilson had heard next to nothing about it. Waaland recalls that Wilson accepted Jones' offer, turned to the Boeing executive next to him and said, "Don't ever let me be in this position again."

The Northrop proposal, code named "Senior Ice," was submitted in December. "It was one of the best proposal efforts I'd been on," says Waaland, "and we ended up feeling pretty buoyant. It was part exhaustion, part fatigue, and part euphoria." By the early spring "we had indications that we had buried the competition."

Lockheed's Senior Peg design is still classified, making a comparison impossible. In his autobiography, Skunk Works leader Ben Rich claimed that the Lockheed design was more stealthy and that Northrop prevailed because of a small edge in aerodynamic performance and because it was a larger aircraft. Cashen disputes that claim. "We had a hell of an aircraft, it's as simple as that. We beat them on the pole, we beat them in the air, we beat them on everything."

As the engineers prepared their final proposals, President Jimmy Carter and many congressional Democrats were defeated by Ronald Reagan and other Republicans in the November 1980 election. Under Carter, several options for renewing the bomber force had been studied. One option was to bring the ATB into service as soon as possible, as a direct replacement for the B-52 and FB-111. Another was to delay the ATB considerably and concentrate on a more stealthy development of the B-1. A third choice, favored in 1979 by SAC commander General Richard Ellis, was to modify existing FB-111As into an interim bomber.

Reagan's defense secretary, Caspar Weinberger, decided on the most expensive option: a full-speed-ahead program to build 100 B-1s in the mid-1980s, followed by 132 stealth bombers. This approach promised to keep SAC viable through 1990, despite projected improvements in Soviet air defenses. It also meant that the U.S. Air Force could spend some time on a risk-reduction program, testing critical technologies for the radical stealth bomber, before committing to a prototype and production program. It was also politically convenient. The Reagan campaign—largely unaware of the existence of stealth—had strongly criticized the cancellation of the B-1 and the new administration was committed to reinstating it.

Northrop was awarded the ATB contract in October 1981, covering full-scale development, preparations for production, and the manufacture of six flying aircraft and two static-test airframes and including options for the production of 127 more bombers (one of the prototypes would not be operational). The contract was worth $36.6 billion in 1981 dollars. The Pentagon wanted to keep the award secret, announcing, for legal reasons, nothing more than the award of a "study" to Northrop. Yet Northrop chairman Tom Jones pointed out that securities law required disclosure of contracts that would materially affect the company's business. A 12-line statement was issued, the last that would be heard of the program, officially, until 1988. The program was code named "Senior CJ" in tribute to Connie Jo Kelly, the indispensable and hardworking secretary to the stealth program office at the Pentagon.

Although Northrop had a contract to build the new bomber, its design was not frozen; and, in fact, it would change dramatically in the first year of the program.

In 1980, in the Pentagon, Paul Kaminski decided to invest 1 percent of the stealth budget in counter-stealth studies. The "Red Team" was divided in two. One group worked with full knowledge of stealth; the other worked from public sources. The effort led to major changes in the bomber design.

The most important lesson was that a stealth aircraft was not invisible. It could and would be detected if its operators did not use tactics that exploited its stealth. The Red Team underscored the importance of planning routes

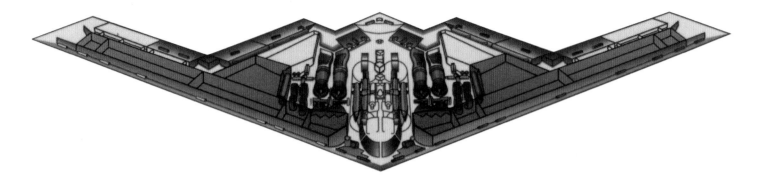

This is the only B-2 impression released so far to show internal details that are often considered sensitive, such as the serpentine exhaust ducts and top-mounted antennas. Also visible, beneath the tail, are the two pitch control/brake surfaces that were part of the initial design. They were wired shut on the early aircraft and removed later in production. *Northrop*

so that the stealth aircraft would show its least visible side to known radars. This led to the development of the first automated mission planning system for the F-117A. Constantly updated with the location of hostile radars, the system devised the stealthiest routes to any chosen target. (Pilots nicknamed it "Elvira," after late-night TV's Mistress of the Dark.) A similar system would be developed to support the ATB.

More significantly, the Red Team suggested that, within the new bomber's service life, the Soviet Union might build large ground-based radars that could overpower stealth technology at a useful range. The Air Force decided to design the bomber so that it could bypass those radars on the deck, using terrain to protect itself.

The design that Northrop submitted for the ATB competition in 1980 was very similar to Hal Markarian's first sketches, apart from being noticeably deeper at the center-section. In response to SAC's indications that it wanted a multimission bomber, the aircraft had grown heavier, with larger weapons bays. This was accomplished within the original planform, at the expense of some altitude performance.

When the Red Team's low-altitude requirement was added to the specification, Northrop initially offered a revised ATB that would fly at Mach 0.55 at low altitude (about the same as the B-52). As the competition entered its final stages, however, it became clear that the bomber would have enough power (because of its low drag) to cruise at Mach 0.8 at low level. Northrop adjusted its final offer to reflect this, while cautioning the Air Force that it had not had time to fully model the aeroelastic effects of the greater gust loads that the aircraft would encounter. Designers expected that they would need to add some local stiffening to the structure, and they would have to change the environmental control system (ECS) to deal with friction heating encountered at high speed and low level.

The issue turned out to be more complex. The designers developed a new computer model that took account of external air loads, the internal structure, and the control laws. All the control surfaces in the original design were located on the slender, flexible outer wings, apart from a gust-alleviation flap on the extreme tail. This placed them ahead of the primary longitudinal bending mode line, which curved across the center-body. In low-altitude turbulence, control movements would tend to bend the whole aircraft across this line as they attempted to counter gust-induced pitch movements. Stiffening the structure would add at least 10,000 pounds (4,500 kilograms) to the empty weight.

Instead, the bomber was redesigned. The outer wings became shorter and thinner and carried only two control segments instead of three. The outboard center-body sections were extended backward, creating the characteristic "double-W" trailing edge, and the exhausts were changed to a V-shape. Two elevon sections were added to each side of the center-body, placing them on a stiffer part of the structure and further aft for greater effectiveness.

At the same time, the RCS group at Northrop produced a different type of radar absorbent structure for the leading edge of the wing, which could provide the required absorption with less depth. This meant that the wing spar and cockpit could be moved forward. The inlets had originally been designed so that part of the duct passed through the spar, with a streamwise vane to help conceal the compressor face from the engine. With the spar moved forward, it was possible to move the entire duct behind the spar and simplify the structural design. The revised aircraft would not only be lighter but would have a better ride at low altitude, so it was possible to eliminate an isolated, palletized cockpit that had been incorporated in the original design.

In 1984, with its redesign complete, the bomber passed an unusual second preliminary design review. The challenge was to build it. This was to prove more difficult than expected, and as always the devil was in the details.

SECRETS BENEATH THE SKIN

Bombers present a unique design challenge, because of their combination of transport-like size and fighter-like intricacy, and the B-2 is an elegantly, densely packed aircraft.

The center-body is little longer than the fuselage of an F-15 but is as deep as a B-52 fuselage, accommodating two large weapon bays, one each side of the centerline. The center-body accommodates the crew compartment, reached through a ventral hatch. The B-2's cockpit windows are so large that they make the aircraft look smaller than it is. They are large for the same reason that the cockpit windows of a DC-10 are large: A cockpit window has to provide the pilot with a given angular field of view, and the further the window is from the pilot's seat, the bigger it has to be. Comparing the location of the ejection-seat hatches with the width of the dorsal hump shows how wide and high the latter is. Even so,

fighter pilots transitioning to the B-2 sometimes feel "that they are trapped in a dumpster" because of the limited field of view, and the nose-down view is limited.

The engines, outboard of the weapon bays, are buried completely within the wing. The S-shaped inlet ducts curve down to the engines, which are accessible from below the aircraft. Curvature conceals the compressor faces from direct line-of-sight illumination by radar, and RAM on the duct walls suppresses any radar energy that could bounce off the duct walls to reach the engines. Ahead of each inlet is a jagged slit-like auxiliary inlet that removes the turbulent boundary layer and provides cool air that is mixed into the exhaust to reduce the bomber's infrared signature. The modern-sculpture shape of the inlets results from the combination of the straight-edge planform alignments with the curvature of the surfaces.

Three B-2s in final assembly at Palmdale in 1990. The aircraft are covered with white protective sheets, and rubber mats are scattered over the upper surfaces to give workers access to the airframe. Assembling such a large aircraft from major assemblies produced in Dallas, Seattle, and Pico Rivera, with the technology in hand in the early 1980s, was a major challenge. *Northrop*

The B-2 is the most perfect embodiment of the flying wing, with only a vestige of a fuselage. The engines are buried completely within the wing: the bulges above the wing are aerodynamic fairings behind the inlets. This is AV-1 in early flight tests, towing an airspeed sensor. The towed sensor was used to back up and validate the new flush air-data system; a conventional probe would have invalidated the latter's readings. *Northrop*

The exhaust ducts have curved profiles. They flatten out to wide slits and open into overwing trenches. As in the case of the F-117, the exhaust system exploits the Coanda effect (the phenomenon that causes spilt water to follow the curved side of a glass rather than falling straight down) to direct the thrust aft while concealing the nozzle openings from a direct rear view.

The B-2's aerodynamic characteristics are unique. Compared with a wing-body design of the same weight, the B-2 has much more span and wing area, so the lift coefficient (a measure of how much lift must be produced by each square foot of wing) does not have to be as high. While conventional aircraft have complex flaps to raise the lift coefficient for takeoff and landing, the B-2 needs none and lifts off at a conservative 140 knots.

Another effect of the big wing is that the B-2 operates over a smaller angle of attack range than a conventional aircraft and flies in a fairly flat, constant attitude regardless of speed and weight. A sophisticated fuel-management system is used for zero-drag trim.

The net result is that the B-2 is very efficient, even though the lift distribution was not what it would be in an ideal flying wing. The B-2 is lighter than the B-1, but has a far better war load and range performance. It can carry about as much and as far as the B-52, which is 50 tons heavier.

The B-2's weight is a curious subject. Early fact sheets gave the maximum takeoff weight as 375,000 pounds (170,500 kilograms). Later, this number was reduced to 336,500 pounds (152,600 kilograms), while other documents place the aircraft "in the 350,000-pounds (158,730-kilogram) class." The current U.S. Air Force Technical Orders quote the 336,500-pound figure. The most probable explanation for this discrepancy is that the bomber's structural life is based on the lowest figure, reflecting a takeoff with full fuel but no weapons. Since a full load has relatively little effect on the bomber's flying qualities, a B-2 will probably never fly with a full load except in combat, which represents a tiny percentage of its lifetime sorties.

Its aerodynamic efficiency is close to that of the Lockheed U-2, a very specialized aircraft with a much smaller design envelope. The B-2's altitude performance is another interesting

Another view of AV-1, early in the flight test program. Two basic principles in the design were to use the lower surface to mask the inlets, exhaust, and cockpit from detection systems beneath the bomber, and to concentrate the mass in the center of the aircraft, where it would be masked from radars at the same level by the gradual slopes of the wing. *Northrop*

The high-flying B-2 is more likely to be illuminated by radar from below than from above, so the lower surface has been made as flat and featureless as possible. The forward center-section, however, is carefully contoured to provide the radar with a good forward field of view. *Northrop*

question: with its great span and wing area, the B-2 is certainly capable of exceeding the nominal 50,000-foot (15,000-meters) ceiling cited in official statements, which is largely determined by the Air Force's normal altitude limit for any aircraft where the crew members do not wear pressure suits.

In most respects, the B-2 is close to neutrally stable. If it had conventional controls, any disturbance would tend to push the aircraft onto a new flight path. It would not diverge farther from its original path unless it was disturbed again, but it would require an action by the pilot to resume its former attitude and speed. Such an aircraft is difficult to hold straight and level, and handling problems of this kind helped persuade the Air Force to prefer conventional designs to the original Northrop flying wings. However, the B-2 is rendered stable and mannerly by a quadruplex fly-by-wire system. The flight control computer units were developed by General Electric, which provided the hardware for the F/A-18 and Tacit Blue. (This General Electric unit is now part of Lockheed Martin.)

The fly-by-wire system drives nine very large control surfaces that occupy the entire trailing edge, apart from the area behind the engines. The outermost pair of surfaces are split horizontally and operate symmetrically, as speed brakes, and asymmetrically as rudders. The flattened, pointed tail of the center-body—known as the gust load alleviation system, or simply the beavertail—is primarily used to counter pitch movements caused by vertical gusts at low level. The remaining six surfaces are elevons for pitch and roll control, although the outermost pair function purely as ailerons at low speed.

Interestingly, two other control surfaces were originally installed beneath the rear of the center-body, just ahead of the beavertail. Apparently intended to pitch the aircraft downward (possibly in the event of an otherwise nonrecoverable stall), the surfaces were never needed. They were wired shut on early aircraft and eliminated completely on later B-2s.

The absence of a vertical fin is one of the B-2's unique features. B-2 designer Irv Waaland describes a conventional aircraft without a vertical fin as "like an arrow without feathers." The flying wing is different, because it is short from front to rear and has no features to generate destabilizing side forces. "The all-wing design is neutrally stable directionally," Waaland says. "All you need is adequate control." Northrop's first designs had small, inward-canted vertical control surfaces on the center-body, immediately outboard of the exhausts. Alternative approaches were evaluated, including a combination of small outboard verticals and reaction controls, before Northrop settled on the brake-rudder surfaces.

The brake-rudders are the primary means of yaw control, but because of the boundary layer over the wing, the surfaces are ineffective until they have moved about 5 degrees from their trail position. The B-2 normally flies with the rudders at "five and five"; that is, slightly displaced so that any movement takes it immediately into a responsive zone. This is not compatible with stealth, so the rudders are closed when the cockpit master mode switch is in its "go to war" position. Instead (according to a 1991 technical paper, although this area is now classified) the B-2 uses differential engine thrust for stealthy directional control.

In side view, the B-2 diminishes to a very small shape, with a fuselage not much longer than that of an F-15. With no flat surfaces or continuous curves, the shape also avoids sharp shadows or strong glints. Steely-eyed fighter pilots who claim to be able to spot hostile aircraft 20 miles away may be disappointed. *Northrop*

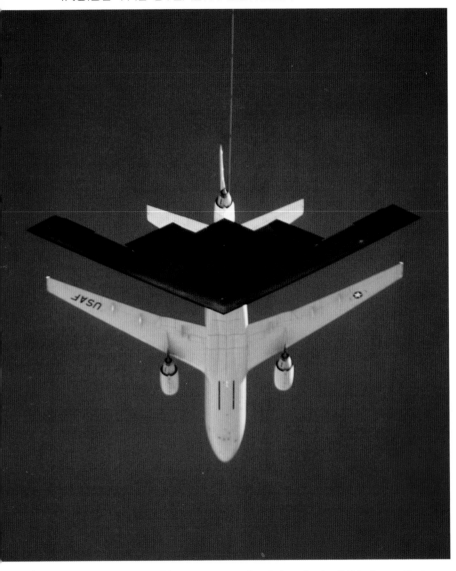

Next to a conventional aircraft, the B-2 looks positively alien. The B-2 has a wingspan 7 feet greater than that of the KC-10 Extender tanker, but its gross weight is less than two-thirds of the tanker's. *Northrop*

The flight control system presented its own challenges. Because the B-2 is short, the elevons have a short moment arm in pitch and must be large to provide adequate power. Being on the wing trailing edge, they are not mass-balanced, so the loads at the hinge line are high. On the other hand, the designers had elected to use the controls to counter gust loads in low-level flight, so the controls had to be able to move very quickly.

To meet these conflicting requirements, Moog and Lear Astronics developed a unique actuation system. The B-2 is fitted with eight actuator remote terminals (ARTs) spread out along the wingspan, which receive their instructions from the GE flight control computers over a quadruplex digital bus. The ARTs issue analog commands to the actuators and control all the necessary feedback loops, saving complexity and weight in the wiring between the FCCs and the actuators. The entire system runs at 4,000 psi to reduce the size and weight of the actuators.

The Rosemount air data system is also new, but proved less troublesome than the air data system on the F-117. (For one agonizing period in the F-117's development, the team was working with several air-data systems, none of which had yet been made to work.) The B-2's system is based on a circular heated port that could measure both normal (static pressure) and pitot pressure. There are five groups of four ports, each arranged on a common pressure line. The system compares pressures at upper and lower ports to determine alpha, and compares left and right ports to determine sideslip.

The B-2 aerodynamic design was primarily based on computational fluid dynamics (CFD), according to aerodynamicist Hans Grellmann,

The B-2's upper and lower surfaces comprise curves of constantly changing radius, avoiding single-curvature surfaces that concentrate radar reflections. The jagged inlet shapes result from the intersection of the plan-view lines and the surface curvature. Boundary-layer air is drawn through the slots ahead of the main inlets and mixed with the exhaust. The dark circular patch to the right of the windshield is the window for the astro-inertial navigation system. *Northrop*

although CFD for whole-airframe design was in its infancy when the program started. "We had to make do with tools that were never designed to do the job," he remarked in a 1990 presentation. A transonic wing analysis code was adapted to define the entire wing. CFD could not directly account for engine flows, so the aerodynamics team subtracted the engine flow from their calculations, leaving only the spilling air-flow. CFD was also used to investigate important handling areas such as in-flight refueling and behavior in ground effect. "We relied on CFD and used the wind tunnel to tell us that our codes were valid," said Grellmann.

Several tunnel models—all produced by numerically controlled machines, driven from the same computer database used in the production of the full-size aircraft—were used for

Clearly visible here are the flush pressure sensors for the Rosemount air-data system, which measures the B-2's speed and altitude by monitoring total and differential pressures around the forebody. One sensor in each group of four is connected to one channel of the flight control system. This view also shows the flight refueling receptacle, which rotates around its long axis to stow within the fuselage. *Northrop*

more than 24,000 hours of total tunnel time. The "workhorse" was a sting-mounted force and moment model with working primary inlets and boundary layer scoops?

Detail design challenges included the need to push the thickness of the center section to the limit of flow separation to accommodate a body depth equal to that of the B-52 in the bomber's 69-foot overall length. The aircraft was also to have conventional pitch and stalling characteristics, even though Cashen's stealth group wanted the leading edge to be as sharp as possible. The wing section itself is a modified NASA laminar-flow profile, rather than a more modern supercritical section, and was chosen because it can combine the camber demanded by cruise aerodynamics with a sharp leading edge.

The leading edge of the wing is a remarkably complex shape, a blend of sharp and blunt edges with changes in camber from root to tip. It evolved as a compromise between aerodynamics and stealth. For a stealth aircraft, the ideal is an infinitely sharp edge, but this would cause flow break-up and excessive drag; the aerodynamicists wanted a smoothly curved edge. The basic compromise was based on the fact that most of the electromagnetic scattering occurred at the ends of each straight leading edge. The resulting edge shape, from the B-2's nose to its wingtips, is like a toothpick: fatter and rounder in the middle and tapering to a point at each end. Toward the nose, to minimize problems of flow separation, the sharp edge is bent downward to align it with the free airstream at the B-2's normal cruising angle of attack, giving the bomber its characteristic hawk's-beak profile.

Northrop selected a new engine from General Electric in the early stages of the ATB contest. It was based on the F101-X, a fighter engine derived from the B-1's engine that later became the F110. Compared with the F101, the F101-X had a smaller low-pressure spool, scaled up from that of the F404, which reduced the bypass ratio from 2:1 to 0.87:1.

Even in 1992, when this photo was taken, two B-2s in the air were a rare sight. The two test aircraft here have their brake/rudders slightly open, matching their acceleration characteristics to those of the tanker and providing the most responsive directional control characteristics. *Northrop*

The F101-X was attractive for two reasons. Although a higher-bypass-ratio engine would be more efficient, it would need a bigger exhaust and inlet system that would add to the bomber's weight, and it would lose thrust more rapidly with altitude. The definitive B-2 engine was originally referred to as F101-F29, but was officially designated F118-GE-100. Compared with the F110, it has a redesigned, higher-airflow fan that provides more non-afterburning power. Its high-altitude potential is indicated by the fact that it has been retrofitted to the Lockheed U-2S.

Inlet design was difficult. The completely flush inlet used on Tacit Blue worked adequately, but experienced starting problems (at one point, the flight test crew borrowed a C-130 to generate airspeed over the Whale's inlet),

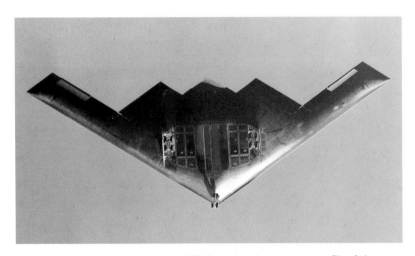

A clear shot of AV-1 shows the concave profile of the lower leading edge and the packaging of landing gear, weapon bays, and engines into the center of the fuselage. The serrated edges of the access doors are visible. *AP/Wide World*

and Northrop was looking for better pressure recovery and efficiency on the bomber. However, the last place to put an efficient inlet is on top of the wing, because a wing generates lift in the form of reduced pressure on its upper surface. The inlet, which is trying to convert the velocity of the incoming air to pressure so that the air can expand out of the exhaust, does not want to ingest low-pressure air.

Although the B-2 is subsonic, its thick supercritical wing sections accelerate the air to supersonic speeds over the wing. The inlet region resembles two supercritical wing sections in series. The first is the area behind the leading edge, where the airflow accelerates to supersonic speed and is then recompressed to subsonic speed before being swallowed by the main inlet and the auxiliary boundary-layer/IR suppression scoop. The second supercritical section comprises the region from the inlet lip to the exhaust exit, where the flow is accelerated and recompressed once again. In cruising flight, the inlet is spilling air (as most inlets do) and the interaction with the flow over the wing translates all the way to the wingtip. Because of this, it was impossible to predict or test the B-2's aerodynamic performance without taking the propulsion system into account.

In the early days of the program, Northrop built a full-scale replica of the inlet, complete with two engines, and tested it on the ground. Only one serious problem turned up: a certain amount of flow separation in the tightly curved duct, leading to a loss of power at low speeds. The solution was to add retractable auxiliary inlet scoops above the wing.

Structurally, the B-2 consists of six major assemblies. The center wing assembly, built by Boeing, contains the weapon bays and the

The split brake-rudders, directly borrowed from the XB-35 and YB-49, are highly effective control surfaces. As they approach their full deflection angles, small covers open to let the hinges pass through the skin. This keeps the rudder gaps small during normal cruising flight while allowing them to open wide at low airspeeds. *Northrop*

avionics bays above and behind them. In front of this is the crew station assembly, produced by Northrop in California. On either side are the two very complex intermediate wing assemblies, which house the inlets, exhausts, engine bays, and main landing gear bays. (The company responsible for these at the start of the program, Vought, has since been acquired by Northrop Grumman.) The outer wings are produced by Boeing, which is also responsible for the weapon launchers and landing gear.

The components of the B-2 actually built by Northrop are only a small proportion of the total weight—the cockpit and the entire perimeter of the aircraft, comprising the leading edges, wingtips, control surfaces, and fixed

A clear view of AV-1 during low-level envelope expansion shows the careful sculpturing of the elevon ends at the apex of the trailing-edge notch. The first concerns about the aft deck have been identified: Instruments have been attached to the skin around the exhaust, connected by scabbed-on external cables to a test-instrument bay in the rear fuselage. *Northrop*

trailing-edge structure. For Northrop, this makes good business sense. Much of the value of a contract resides in the design, the integration (which includes the cockpit), and the use of company-proprietary technology, such as the radar-absorbent edges of a stealth aircraft.

Inside the center and intermediate wing sections are two very large titanium carry-through box (CTB) structures, one behind the cockpit and the other one aft of the engine bay. Otherwise, the primary structural material is carbonfibre/epoxy composite, which is used for most of the skin and the spars of the outer wing. The B-2 includes many of the largest carbonfibre parts ever made, including center-section skins that are more than 1 inch (2.5 centimeters) thick and spars and skins more than 70 feet long, and it is still by far the largest aircraft ever built primarily from composite material.

One of the most important reasons for choosing the new material had to do with stealth. Carbonfibre is less dense than metal, so carbonfibre skins are thicker than metal skins of the same strength, and composite parts can be assembled by "co-curing" them: autoclaving them together, so that the parts bond together with a strength equal to that of the original material. Most of the stiffeners are co-cured to the skins.

The thick, fastener-free skins produced by this method are smoother than riveted metal skins and will stay that way in service, a characteristic that was critical to Northrop's "seamless" stealth design technique. The large skin panels reduced the number of structural joints, which were possible sources of unwanted radar reflections.

The result was a durable and relatively simple structural design; the question was whether anyone could draw it, let alone build it.

The B-2's windshield is huge, but the crew sits well behind it and the view from the cockpit is limited. The B-2 was built with a third crew station, in case the crew workload made it necessary—the dotted outline of the ejection hatch is visible—but this has not been used either in flight test or in operations. The diamond-shaped patch on the leading edge, to the left of the seam in the leading-edge RAM assembly, may cover an antenna for the defensive management system. *Northrop*

Northrop's stealth design philosophy, with its continuous flowing curves, had worked on the hand-built Tacit Blue prototype, but a large mass-produced bomber was a different matter. Most aircraft are built from the inside out, starting with spars, ribs, and frames. These are all parts that are defined in two dimensions

Among the unpleasant surprises encountered in the first phase of the B-2 program was the realization that the bomber would have to be made from more sophisticated, more expensive composite materials than the designers had expected. Composite parts that might be an inch thick and contain hundreds of plies were produced by laying up the parts in a mold and placing them in a pressure oven, or autoclave. The autoclave would melt the epoxy resin and force it into any voids in the part. This massive autoclave was installed by Vought in 1989 for the B-2 production program. *Vought*

and assembled into the complete structure. Any deviations from the design accumulate into small errors in fit and surface finish, which are fixed during final assembly. Cumulatively, the errors are usually bigger on large aircraft. The result is that the external surface does not exactly resemble the drawings.

The B-2 could not be built this way. One critical issue was that the effect of gaps or steps in the skin was determined by the grazing angle between the incoming radar wave and the skin. Like shadows close to sunset, this effect was much greater at shallow grazing angles, and most of the B-2's surfaces presented such angles to the incoming waves. On an aircraft as big as the B-2, it was impractical to overcome the problem by coating the entire airplane with radar absorbent material (RAM). The only answer was to make the major skin panels fit almost perfectly, so that there would be no gaps or steps even when the aircraft was pummelled and bent by turbulence. But the classic methods of ensuring that parts conformed to the design shape were inadequate, being basically designed for single-curvature surfaces.

Since stealth was a critical aspect of the design and would have to be demonstrated by the first B-2s, the first aircraft off the line would have to be exactly the same in every external detail as all the others; that is to say, it would be built on hard tooling. But this tooling would have to be installed and aligned to unprecedented standards of accuracy before the first bomber was built.

The solution was twofold. First, the B-2 would be defined and built from the outside in. Instead of being made of flexible sheets fastened to substructure, the skin panels would be laid up in precise female molds. Second, to make sure that everything would fit, the entire aircraft would be designed on computers.

As the company renovated the massive Ford automobile plant at Pico Rivera, west of Los Angeles, where much of the B-2 was to be built, it did so according to a new concept: computer integrated manufacturing. At Pico Rivera, the image of computer-aided design became the reality. The external shape of the new bomber was defined on a computer database, not in terms of sections and stations, but in its totality. The database would define the precise three-dimensional coordinates of any point on the skin. The database was housed on banks of tape drives and managed by a Cray supercomputer.

Connected to the database were more than 400 computer work stations at Pico Rivera. The database was shared with major subcontractors Boeing and Vought and their own engineers. As detail design proceeded, the engineers could work from the outside in; as the design of each part was completed, it was added to the database. The computer system grew to define the shape and location of every component of the B-2, quite literally down to the smallest fastener.

Early in the program, the database took over from the first "engineering fixture" produced to support the B-2 design, so that the aircraft became the first to be created without a true mock-up. Computer-aided design is standard practice now, but it was far from being so in 1983, and the Northrop team found itself breaking new ground—with the aid of computer technology which, by today's standards, was quite primitive. Even with computer integrated manufacturing, the internal plumbing and wiring of AV-1, the first aircraft, proved to be a voracious consumer of man hours.

Materials were another problem. The skin had to be made thicker and heavier than predicted, because its stealth characteristics might be compromised if it buckled under loads. Other requirements compounded the problem.

One of the principal ways to reduce the cost of building and maintaining stealth-compatible apertures is to minimize their number. On the B-2, ground-based electrical and air connections are made through the nose landing gear bay (as seen here) and the pressure refueling points are in the main gear bays.
James C. Goodall

Apertures are a design problem on a stealthy aircraft, particularly when they have to open and close in flight. The nose landing gear doors and crew access door have overlapping edges, scalloped seals, and complex positive locks to ensure that they do not gap under flight loads.
James C. Goodall

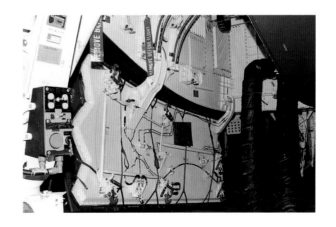

The "toothpick" profile of the leading edge—with a large radius at the middle and a small radius at each end—is very apparent in this view. From an RCS standpoint, a sharp edge is best, but the aerodynamic penalty would be unacceptable. The compromise was to design a leading edge that was blunt at its midpoint but sharp at the ends, where RCS issues were most important. *James C. Goodall*

Waaland says: "We entered the program with what we thought was a full range of validated materials, both low-observable and non–low-observable. We were required to validate our materials for nuclear flash and dust, long-life ultraviolet exposure, rain, supportability, producibility, and a lot of other concerns. The bottom line is that nothing that we started with survived."

Before the first B-2 was completed, Northrop and its teammates tested more than 900 materials. Where the chosen approach seemed risky, the customer demanded extensive demonstrations. For example, three complete 15-meter composite wing skin panels were built in 1982 and 1983 before the Air Force was satisfied that the material would be durable, that there would be no problems with lightning, and that the promised 7,000-pound weight saving would be achieved. Only then could Northrop and Boeing cease working on a back-up aluminum-alloy design.

In many cases, new materials not only cost money to develop, but were more expensive in production as well. The basic epoxy resins used in early composite structures were prone to "delamination"—the resin bond between the plies of fabric was brittle, and gaps developed over time and after impact damage, causing invisible weaknesses in the fabric. Like other manufacturers, Northrop had to switch from early epoxy resins to new formulations that offered better through-the-skin toughness and resisted delamination better. Around the engines, epoxies gave way to new heat-tolerant bismaleimide and polyimide resins. Many of these materials and processes have or will become standard on later programs, spreading through Northrop's partners and subcontractors.

The third principal driver behind the B-2 design, along with aerodynamics and structures, was stealth technology. The concept of "balanced observables" is essential to understanding the design of a stealth aircraft. In the ideal "balanced" aircraft, the range at which it will be detected in any spectrum—radar, infrared, visual, or acoustic—will be much the same.

RCS reduction is the most critical element of stealth, because radar provides the defender with the most information at the longest range. Denys Overholser, one of the key players in the Lockheed Have Blue design, lists the four most important factors in RCS reduction as "shape, shape, shape, and materials." Shape is by far the biggest factor in reducing RCS, but special radar-absorbent material (RAM) is necessary to mop up residual scattering from the shaped surfaces and to suppress reflections from features such as inlets, which cannot be totally stealthy in their basic design. RAM is applied to an existing structure and adds to its weight without increasing its strength; radar-absorbing structure (RAS) involves building these materials into load-bearing structure.

Most of the B-2 is covered by multilayer sprayed-on elastomeric coatings that maintain a uniform conductivity at the surface. RAM is used selectively in areas such as control-surface gaps, doors and other apertures, and inside the inlet ducts.

RAM consists of an active element—a material such as carbonyl iron particles, which transform radar energy into heat—embedded in a dielectric plastic matrix. It is usually formulated and applied so that the small reflection from the front face of the absorber is canceled by a residual reflection from the structure beneath it. The basic technique is to make the total pathway of energy within the RAM equal to half a wavelength, so that the residual reflection is exactly out-of-phase with the front-face reflection. The RAM can be much thinner than the nominal wavelength of the radar and still achieve cancellation, because the wavelength inside the material is much shorter than it is in free space.

Solid RAM coatings cover a frequency range of about 20:1. This is enough to address air-to-air and surface-to-air missile radars (from the L-band up to the Ku-band), but more elaborate schemes are used to cover the full radar spectrum, which includes VHF radars with wavelengths of almost 2 meters.

While the leading edges of the B-2 cannot be described in detail, a wide-band radar absorbent structure (RAS), used on the edges of a stealth aircraft, has been compared to a stereo system with a "tweeter" and a "woofer." The "tweeter" is a high-frequency ferromagnetic absorber, applied over a resistive layer that reflects higher frequencies but allows low-frequency signals to pass through. Beneath this resistive layer is the low-frequency "woofer": a glass-fiber honeycomb core, treated from front to back with a steadily increasing amount of resistant material. Behind this is a sharp-edged, wedge-section reflective surface. What little energy reaches this surface will be attenuated once again before it escapes from the absorber.

The need to reduce RCS can make simple features hard to design. The unconventional Rosemount air-data system is needed because a normal pitot probe, with a forward-facing cavity, has an inherently large RCS. Antennas have to be buried in treated, specially shaped

Inlet design was one of the most difficult jobs on the B-2, because of the interaction between the inlet and the airflow over the wing. The radar-absorbent liner of the left inlet duct is just visible here. Northrop felt that lined S-ducts were preferable to gridded or baffled inlets. *Bill Sweetman*

The B-2's main landing gear is similar to that of the General Dynamics B-58. The legs retract forward and a large drag link efficiently passes braking loads into the structure. The nose landing gear is longer than it seems at first sight and retracts rearward. *Bill Sweetman*

cavities, behind covers that block all signals except the exact frequency used by that antenna.

Because access panels have to be treated so carefully, it is best to eliminate as many of them as possible. This involves careful design. On the B-2, one panel usually gives access to several systems. Other subsystems, such as the avionics, are installed so that they can be reached through existing apertures such as the crew boarding hatch, weapons bay, and landing gear bay. The B-2 is also unusual in that it has no drain holes. Instead, drain paths lead to collector sumps that can be emptied on the ground by pushing a panel inward.

After radar, infrared systems have the greatest potential range of any sensor. There are many types of infrared sensors in service, and their different capabilities are sometimes confused. At a range of a few miles, a small infrared sensor can receive enough energy to produce a TV-type image of the target, but this capability diminishes quickly with range.

Longer-range infrared sensors, such as the infrared search and track systems (IRSTS) fitted to fighters and the homing heads of infrared-guided missiles, do not usually detect the infrared emissions from the aircraft itself, but the radiation from the hot gas and water vapor emitted by its engines. The stealth designer's first task in the infrared spectrum is therefore to deal with the exhausts.

The B-2's exhausts are built into the top of the wing. The primary nozzles are well ahead of the trailing edge and lead into a pair of soft-lipped trenches that flare outward. The engines are fitted with flow mixers to blend the cold bypass air with the hot core stream. The cold boundary layer, which is swallowed by the secondary inlets, is injected into the exhaust stream to cool it further. The exhausts are wide and flat, so the perimeter of the plume is longer than the perimeter of a round exhaust stream, and mixing takes place more quickly. Finally, the interaction between the exhaust stream and the airflow over the aircraft, at each angled side of the exhaust "trench," creates a vortex that further promotes mixing.

At shorter ranges, infrared systems detect radiation from the aircraft's skin. This is produced in two ways: from reflected sunlight and skin friction. Infrared absorbent paints are widely used. Containing compounds such as zinc sulfide, they work exactly like paints with visual colors, absorbing energy in a certain waveband. In this case, they absorb infrared radiation from sunlight.

Heat generated by skin friction cannot be affected by an absorbing paint, but coatings have been developed that change the "emissivity" of the surface; that is, the efficiency with which it converts heat into infrared radiation. Only certain bands of infrared radiation travel efficiently through the atmosphere, so if the aircraft is coated with a substance that can shift energy into a different band, an infrared detector may not be able to see it. Infrared emissions can also be reduced by slowing down or climbing into thinner air, both of which a B-2, with its modest wing loading, can do.

The most conspicuous element of the visual signature is not part of the aircraft but its contrail. Contrails can be suppressed by changing altitude, if the pilot knows they are there. In 1994, Northrop Grumman filed a patent for a lidar (laser radar) system which would measure the reflection of a laser beam behind the aircraft and determine the size of the particles in the exhaust. Particle size is the main factor influencing

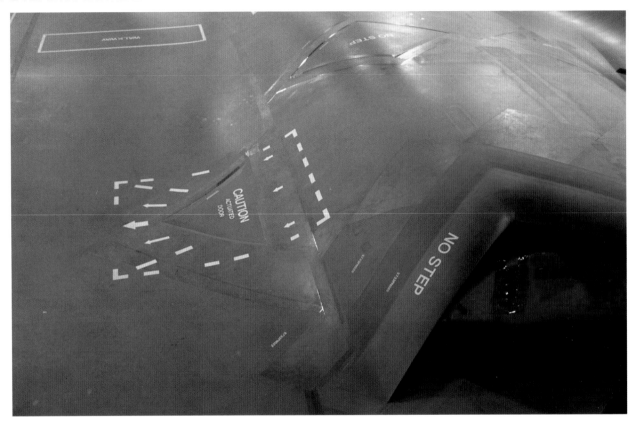

The AlliedSignal APU is installed outboard of the starboard engine bay. The inlet is presumably buried inside the main inlet duct, and the exhaust is concealed by a small triangular panel. *James C. Goodall*

whether or not contrails are visible. This system was tested on a NASA F/A-18.

Contrails can be made less visible by injecting chemicals into the exhaust that break the water into droplets smaller than the wavelength of visible light. In the 1960s, the U.S. Air Force tested a system that injected chloro-flouro-sulfonic acid (CSA) into the exhaust stream on B-47 and B-52 bombers. CSA is toxic and corrosive and was abandoned in favor of a newer, still classified system that is in use on the B-2 and F-117. One alternative in the open literature is an alcohol/surfactant mixture. According to a General Accounting Office report, a new contrail management system is part of the B-2 Block 30 upgrade.

Because the B-2's underside is a dark gray, people tend to think that it is intended to fight only at night. This is unlikely, because the B-2 was designed to bomb the Soviet Union, and the direct route from the central United States to central Russia lies smack across the Arctic Circle where it is daylight 24 hours a day for a large part of the year.

Altitude is critical to visual signature. An airliner at its cruising height always appears brightly lit against the sky, regardless of whether it is finished in American's bare metal or United's formal gray. This is because both the aircraft and the sky above it are illuminated by light that is scattered by dust and moisture in the air. There is not much of either in the thin air above the aircraft and lots of both below it.

The higher the aircraft flies, the more light is scattered onto its underside and the darker the sky behind it. The B-2's undersides are dark because it cruises at altitudes as high as 50,000 feet, where a dark gray blends into the sky. It would not be surprising if the B-2 had an upward-facing light sensor that would instruct the pilot to increase or reduce altitude slightly to match the changing luminance of the sky.

Again, the goal is not to be invisible, but to be so hard to detect that no reliable and affordable detection scheme can be found. The sharpest fighter pilot has a hard time seeing another aircraft more than 5 nautical miles away, absent a contrail or a "cue" from another sensor. The B-2 is likely to be at least 2 miles away from any loitering fighter in the vertical plane alone, which also reduces the chance that it will be backlit against the horizon.

The Red Team studied, built, and tested acoustic detection devices and determined that they did not present a threat to high-altitude aircraft. Even the quietest places on earth have too much background noise to permit high-flying aircraft to be detected.

Finally, there is one signature that exceeds the range of radar and provides even better identification: emissions from the aircraft's own systems. Stealth has been a major influence on the design, manufacture, and cost of the B-2's mission avionics, which are designed to detect, identify, and locate virtually any large surface target with no outside help, under any weather conditions—something which no other aircraft can do.

The system is managed by the B-2's two-member crew. Both are rated pilots: The pilot occupies the left seat, and the mission commander sits on the right and has primary responsibility for navigation and weapon delivery. Behind the crew station is an area shared by avionics racks and space for a third crew station.

The cockpit is designed so that either crew member can perform the complete mission. Each pilot has four 6-inch-square, full-color cathode-ray-tube (CRT) cockpit displays arranged in a T shape. These can display flight information, sensor inputs, or systems data on command. Each pilot also has a data entry panel to his right and a set of throttles to his left. (The throttles, like the flight controls, are linked electronically to the engines.) There is also a set of "master mode switches" that configure the displays and computers for preflight, takeoff, cruise, and landing.

The space for a third seat, well behind the pilots' seats, was retained in case the workload proved too great. As it was, more than 6,000 hours of manned simulation had been carried out before the B-2 was unveiled, convincing SAC that two pilots would be enough.

The B-2's roomy "glass cockpit" has full controls for both crew members. It has central control sticks, because the fly-by-wire flight control system does not require two-hand inputs. Both pilots have left-hand throttles and a right-hand data entry panel (DEP) to program onboard computers. There are four 6-inch-square, full-color multi-purpose display unit (MDU) screens on each side and a central engine performance monitor (EPM) screen. The "master mode" switches automatically configure the displays for takeoff and landing, cruise and combat. *Northrop*

The primary functions of the mission avionics are navigation, target detection, and self-defense. The navigation subsystem initially combined two units, either of which is capable of navigating the aircraft on its own but which are most accurate and reliable when they work together. One of them is an inertial measurement unit from Kearfott, and the other is a Northrop NAS-26 astro-inertial unit. Northrop pioneered this technology in the early 1950s when it developed the Snark long-range cruise missile.

The astro-inertial system developed for the Snark was based on a stabilized electro-optical telescope, capable of locking on to a preselected star, even in cloudy daylight. A version of this system was used on the A-12 and SR-71, and an improved descendant is fitted to the B-2, with an observation port to the left of the windshield.

The Block 20 upgrade to the B-2 includes a Global Positioning System (GPS) receiver, with a specially developed low-observable antenna. GPS equals or surpasses the accuracy of the astro-inertial unit and will replace it in routine operations, although the astro-inertial unit will remain in use as an unjammable backup.

The B-2's APQ-181 radar (known as the radar subsystem or RSS) was originally developed by the Radar Systems Group of GM-Hughes Electronics. It is now a Raytheon Systems product following that company's takeover of Hughes. In the early days of the program, B-2 critics often complained that the bomber would have no way of finding its targets at long standoff ranges without betraying its presence by radar emissions. This argument was a measure of the effectiveness of the security that protected the development of low-probability-of-intercept (LPI) radar technology over many years. By the time the B-2 development program started in 1981, Hughes and Northrop had been actively developing LPI airborne radar for more than three years under the Tacit Blue program.

The basic principle of LPI is to emit the least amount of energy required to detect and track the target, while manipulating the signal to make it difficult for an adversary to detect it among all the electronic burps, honks, and squeals that pollute the high-tech battlefield. LPI techniques include the adaptive management of power—the radar gradually increases its power until it sees a target and then holds its power level or reduces it as the range declines—and constant variations in frequency and waveform. LPI antennas are designed so that they have very small sidelobes (signals emitted on either side of the main beam) so that emissions are confined to a narrow beam.

The APQ-181 has two 585-pound (265-kilogram) electronically scanned antennas built into the lower leading edge of the wing, one on each side. Each radar antenna has its own power supply, transmitter/receiver, and signal processing unit. The two chains are cross-connected so that the radar can continue to perform even if part of one chain fails.

The radar operates in the Ku-band (12-18 GHz), which is a higher frequency and shorter wavelength than the X-band (around 10 GHz), where most airborne radars operate. Ku-band radars suffer from more atmospheric absorption than X-band and are less suitable for large-area searches because, all other things being equal, they require more power and more time to scan a given volume. They have inherently higher resolution than X-band radars, however, and for a given antenna size, a Ku-band radar will have smaller and weaker sidelobes that will dissipate more quickly.

Among the most important of the radar's 20 modes are a synthetic aperture radar (SAR) mode and terrain following and terrain avoidance (TF/TA). The latter modes provide data to dual TF/TA processors that interface with the flight control system, allowing the B-2 to fly at low level under automatic control in any conditions. The radar has a ground moving target indication (GMTI) mode to detect vehicles on the ground, and an LPI air-to-air mode that may be used during in-flight refueling as well as more conventional long-range mapping and weather modes.

Radar development proved difficult and expensive. The first experimental radar antenna in the program flatly refused to transmit a coherent beam. The problem caused near-panic in the program office, but it was soon realized that it was due to leakage among the ports in the electronically scanned antenna: the antenna was not built to sufficiently tight tolerances. Each antenna included more than 400 precision machined parts with a total of 600,000 high-tolerance features. Among those parts were 85 "phasor plates," machined from a solid slab of magnesium alloy in a cutting process during which the machine head moves 6.4 kilometers. Using conventional machining, each plate would take 25 hours of cutting work, which meant that one machine working regular hours would take two years to build this single part for one aircraft.

Hughes addressed the problem by introducing the emerging technology of high-speed machining, with cutter heads rotating at 25,000 to 75,000 rpm. This reduced the machining time to 4.5 hours for each of the plates, making the manufacture of the APQ-181 antenna practicable if still not exactly cheap. This was the first use of high-speed machining in aerospace, and it has since proved itself into a variety of applications

The third main element of the B-2 mission avionics is the defensive management subsystem. Details of the defensive management subsystem, which includes components from Lockheed Martin, Raytheon, and Honeywell, are largely classified. Its most important element, however, appears to be the Lockheed Martin (formerly Loral, and before that, IBM) APR-50, which has also been identified by the internal designation ZSR-63.

The ZSR-63 replaced an earlier Northrop-developed system called ZSR-62, which was abandoned after encountering development problems. As far as is known, this was the only major subsystem to be scrapped during development, a measure of the difficulty of the defensive management subsystem task. All details of the problems with the ZSR-62 remain secret.

One firmly unanswered question is whether the B-2 has ever been intended to use active cancellation, a stealth technique in which the aircraft detects an incoming signal, copies it, and transmits a canceling or nulling signal. The canceling signal has the same frequency as the original radar emission, but is a half-wavelength out of phase (the same principle is used in active noise reduction for cars and aircraft) so that the radar sees nothing. The challenge in active cancellation is to make it work only when it is needed, with no more power than is absolutely necessary, so that it does not act as a beacon. It is probably impossible to achieve on a nonstealthy aircraft, with a very complex pattern of strong returns, but it may be a practical way to eliminate residual reflections on a stealth aircraft, where the pattern of radar reflections is weaker and simpler. The U.S. Air Force has stated that the B-2's defensive systems are entirely passive, but this begs the question of whether active cancellation has been considered as an upgrade or whether it was part of the canceled ZSR-62.

The APR-50 is designed to detect, classify, identify, and locate hostile systems that emit radio-frequency energy. While the B-2's mission can be preplanned to present the aircraft's least detectable aspects to known threats, there is always the risk that some radars have been moved or have not been detected before the mission. The APR-50, which has been compared to the electronic surveillance measures capability of a dedicated electronic warfare aircraft such as the EA-6B, provides the B-2 crew with real-time updates. It consists of an automated signal-processing and analysis system linked to receiver antennae distributed across the airframe.

In combat, the B-2's information management system and cockpit displays should be able to "fuse" data from many sources. Radar imagery, for example, will be superimposed on maps of the target area, acquired by satellite and stored on board the B-2. The physical and electronic characteristics of known threats can also be stored and fused. If an SA-5 radar is detected, the system can display its location, its predicted area of coverage, and the bomber's projected track on the CRT; the crew can determine instantly whether a course change is necessary.

Much of the avionics system is based on 13 common avionics control unit processors (built by a former Unisys unit that is now part of Lockheed Martin), which carry out several functions that, in earlier systems, were performed by special-purpose computers: TF/TA, navigation, defensive systems, and stores management are all carried out by avionics control units. Designed to stringent requirements for radiation-hardening and vibration tolerance (some of them are installed in the aft center-body,

The B-2 weapon system trainer was one of the world's most sophisticated simulators at the time of its introduction. (It was developed by Link, but after a series of mergers, Raytheon now runs the program.) Particularly challenging features included the need to replicate the B-2's radar display and defensive management system, accurately reproducing the way that they would respond to real-world targets and threats. *Northrop*

between the engine exhausts), the avionics control units can be expanded to handle more complex processing tasks through new software.

The navigation and radar systems have been tested on a modified Boeing C-135 transport, known as the flight-test avionics laboratory (FTAL), which made its first flight in January 1987. The FTAL was needed because many radar modes cannot be adequately tested

South Carolina was delivered to the Air Force on December 29, 1994 as a Block 10 aircraft, and it arrived at Whiteman AFB a day later. In April 1998 it was upgraded to Block 30 standard, incorporating improvements including a further radar signature reduction, new radar modes, enhanced terrain-following capability, a contrail management system, and the ability to deliver additional weapons.

on a static test rig and some (such as SAR) cannot be demonstrated at all except in the air.

These were only the most obvious ways in which the B-2 was expected to advance the state of the art in aerospace, but there were others, some of which are still classified. As the B-2 requirement was being defined in the early 1980s, the customer was well aware that the B-2 would be the last new bomber for a long time. With strong support from those members of Congress who were permitted to know about stealth, and encouragement from a hawkish administration, the U.S. Air Force wrote the toughest set of requirements ever seen. "In the requirements stage, money was no object," one engineer recalls.

Since the bombers and submarines might be the only surviving element of the U.S. nuclear strike force, the ATB was designed to be recovered and reconstituted. After their first nuclear mission, the bombers would return to the United States and land at dispersal airfields (the B-2 can operate from any airfield that can handle a Boeing 727), where they could be rearmed and launched on a second strike. No previous bomber, including the B-1, was designed to meet such a requirement. It meant not only that the bomber needed a high level of reliability and redundancy, but that every part of the aircraft had to be radiation-hardened to an unprecedented degree to survive the blasts of radiation from its own nuclear bombs and from Soviet nuclear air-defense warheads. Even mundane components like the Tacan receiver had to be specially designed. "About the only thing that was not rad-hardened was the antiskid system," Waaland recalled.

When it came to deciding how to meet these requirements, the Air Force and civilian engineers worked closely together, but in a management system that, program participants recall, did not allow them to see how their decisions affected the cost "There was a lack of cost information to the engineers," Waaland says. "If the engineers are left unchecked, they will always go for the best solution." One example was as simple as the radio: From the early stages of the program, it was decided that the ATB should have an advanced antijam radio. "After we put it in the aircraft," says Waaland, "we had nobody to talk to, because apart from the B-2 the program had been cancelled."

Moreover, there are features of the aircraft that apparently have not been discussed at all. "From the beginning, it was the Advanced Technology Bomber," one insider notes, "not just the Stealth bomber. That's where the money is, not in the stealth. There are certain special technologies that cost a fortune."

More than 15 years after the B-2 was designed, it is interesting to ask how many other combat aircraft in service have multimode LPI radars, how many incorporate what can almost be classed as a signals intelligence system, how many use differential thrust for control, and how many are primarily built from composite materials. The answer to these and many similar questions is Big Fat Zero. Little wonder, then, that the B-2 development was not easy.

NOBODY SAID THIS WOULD BE EASY

As these words were written, the B-2 was still some months away from being declared fully operational. Quite clearly, there were delays in the program, along with the cost overruns that inevitably accompany such delays. Pervasive secrecy has made it extremely difficult to put the entire story of the program together. Even what follows is a preliminary account of a story that remains very sensitive, for reasons of politics and national security.

When the B-2 program started, in October 1981, the first aircraft was planned to fly around the end of 1987. By that time, a concurrent production program would be underway, with the rate increasing as the "learning curve" took effect. The bomber would attain an initial operating capability in 1991 or 1992; around then, the production rate would attain a peak of 30 aircraft per year.

A common factor in almost any project that runs late is excessive optimism at the outset, and the B-2 was no exception. In a 1996 interview, Dr. Paul Kaminski noted that hopes for stealth were high when the B-2 started. "The success of the F-117 had set up expectations. It was a given that we could achieve everything that we could do on the F-117, while eliminating all its deficiencies and limitations; but it wasn't just like falling off a log."

From the start, the B-2 was affected by the progress of the B-1B program. In fact, work on the B-2 was quite slow for the first year, because the B-1B was "ramping up" so quickly and absorbing most of the available money. Most of that time was taken up with the wing redesign; by extensive penetration studies, to validate the basic principles of the design; and by a lengthy study of the two-versus-three-crew issue.

The Block 30 modification is a major program. These aircraft have been stripped to their black carbonfibre skins. Leading edges and trailing-edge controls have been removed from both aircraft and will be replaced by new units with better LO characteristics. Close to the camera, the bare metal of the titanium-alloy exhaust trench can be seen at the edge of the red protective matting. The apparent step in the exhaust, just ahead of the wing trailing edge, will be filled in with RAM. *Northrop*

Approximately $1 billion was spent on the early stages of B-2 development to design hardware and software that would define the aircraft as a computer database. The B-2 was the first aircraft of anything like its size and complexity to be defined and built without a solid mock-up. Today, this is standard throughout the industry, and powerful computer-aided design systems run on computers that are little larger than home PCs. *Northrop*

The target first-flight and initial operating capability dates did not change during 1983, however, despite the fact that the wing redesign put the program about a year behind where it was expected to be. The reason was in large measure political. Rockwell, teamed with Lockheed, was still actively promoting a follow-on version of the B-1B, and there was some concern that delays in the B-2 program, acknowledged so early in its life, would make an improved B-1 more attractive.

The Air Force was concerned about technical risks and set up a "risk closure" program in which large-scale tests (such as the full-scale inlet rig) were used in an attempt to identify and solve problems before they could manifest themselves on the full-size aircraft. Designer Irv Waaland calls it "the world's most complete R&D program. There was a belief that nothing should go untested."

This philosophy was sustained throughout the program. To this day, it ensures that what is delivered to the user actually works as advertised, but it does not foster rapid progress.

Security was a larger-than-expected factor in the cost of the program. Have Blue and Tacit Blue were developed in strict secrecy, but they were smaller programs. They were developed by small, hand-picked teams, and as few people as possible were told that they existed. The companies did not need to hire new people to build the aircraft, and many components were bought off-the-shelf from outside suppliers who did not need to know what their products were being used for. Even the F-117 used many off-the-shelf parts.

On those programs "we protected the perimeters," says Waaland. "We researched people, investigated, and did background checks, but information within the program was free-flowing. On the B-2, we introduced total accountability for everything." At any time, the Air Force expected to be able to ask for the location of any document in the program. "It really added costs and reduced productivity," Waaland said.

Secrecy, on the B-2, "had many nonbeneficial aspects," Kaminski says now. The project's classification level meant that the most stringent regulations had to be put into effect over literally thousands of subcontractors. Tens of thousands of newly hired people had to be vetted for security and tested for drug use (this in Los Angeles, in the early 1980s). The vetting system was swamped, and many employees spent weeks in limbo, on the payroll but unable to work. Overall, secrecy added 10 to 15 percent to the cost of the program.

Together with the technical challenges in every area—manufacturing, controls, avionics—these measures drove costs up and caused delay. Since no schedule had been published, however, and since the project was shrouded in secrecy, public criticism was muted, at least for a time.

The B-2 emerged from the black on November 22, 1988, when AV-1 was unveiled at Palmdale. Invited guests were allowed to view only the front of the bomber, and no pictures of the plan-view were released (a security measure that failed to deter *Aviation Week*'s Mike Dornheim, who flew a photographer over the rollout site, above the minimum altitude set by the FAA, and secured clear shots of the plan-view shape and exhaust nozzles).

By this time, the program was drawing more criticism from the media and from politicians. The fact that the production and service-entry schedule was still secret tended to heighten speculation that there were serious problems with the B-2. In fact, the program was running 18 to 24 months behind the original schedule, and AV-1 was far from ready to fly: many internal parts had not been installed when it rolled out.

There were understandable reasons behind the delays. The bomber had undergone a major redesign, it was breaking ground in many areas, and the program philosophy favored completeness over schedule. But these

B-2s on the production line at Palmdale. The smooth external finish of the first aircraft is apparent. The bare skin has a greenish color, possibly indicating that an outer ply—perhaps designed to resist electromagnetic pulse (EMP) or as part of the LO treatment— is bonded to the skin during manufacture. Carbonfibre components are usually soot black. *Northrop*

Apart from being a perfectly timed photograph of the B-2's roll-out, just as the flag above the hangar doors was reflected in the windshield, this view clearly shows the way in which the bomber's surface contours comprise continuous spiral curves, with no creases and few curves of constant radius. *Northrop*

were all secret, so the public and the media were left to draw their own conclusions as the winter of 1988 turned to the summer of 1989.

Finally, AV-1 took to the air on July 17, 1989. A 2-hour, 20-minute first flight was made from Palmdale to Edwards Air Force Base in California. Pilots were Bruce Hinds, chief test pilot for the Northrop B-2 Division, and Colonel Richard Couch, commander of the B-2 Combined Test Force at Edwards. The landing gear remained extended, and observers remarked on the aircraft's almost unnatural steadiness on the approach.

But by June 1990, AV-1 had flown only 16 times, for some 67 hours. There was one mechanical problem, cracking in the aircraft mounted accessory drive (AMAD) casings, but

it was anticipated as a result of earlier tests and was solved fairly quickly. AV-2 was still in final assembly and would not fly until October 19.

Scepticism about the management of Air Force programs in general, and bombers in particular, was fostered by intractable problems with the B-1B's defensive avionics system. Ironically, the root of these problems was that crucial tests had not been performed before the design was committed to production, in direct contrast to the cause of the B-2 delays.

Nevertheless, Congress became reluctant to commit the B-2 to production until flight tests were well advanced. Representative Les Aspin, the Wisconsin Democrat who chaired the House Armed Services Committee, used his committee to delay full-rate production.

Under the original plan, B-2 production should have picked up pace in the fiscal year 1988–1989 budgets. B-2s could be delivered 60 months after being ordered, putting large-scale deliveries and full operational capability in 1994–1995. But Congress refused to appropriate the money. First, Congress delayed the start of production to take account of the late start of flight-testing. Then, in the summer of 1989, Congress mandated that certain flight tests, including the first stage of observables testing, should be completed before full-rate production could begin.

The impact on the program was massive. Northrop and the U.S. Air Force had not planned to perform full RCS tests so early. AV-1, the first aircraft, would not be ready to perform the full RCS tests until late 1990, and they would not be complete until the summer of 1991. Until then, Congress would not authorize procurement beyond the 11 B-2s already under contract: six development aircraft and five production aircraft, the last of which would not be delivered until late 1994. Long-lead items for five more B-2s were authorized, but these aircraft would not be ready until 1995. Even with these aircraft, however, the Air Force would not have enough production aircraft to form a squadron.

The B-2 was a complex airplane, and each aircraft took five years from the start of work to delivery. Therefore, even if the RCS tests went perfectly, full-rate production deliveries could not start until 1996, so the aircraft could not be operational until late 1996 at the earliest.

Also, preparations for production were well underway, and more than 40,000 people were working on the B-2 program. Suspending production would have had a catastrophic

The first B-2, minutes after its public unveiling in November 1988. At this time, the aircraft was far from ready to fly, lacking engines and major system components. After the roll-out, the B-2 went back into its hangar and did not re-emerge until the summer of 1989. *Bill Sweetman*

impact; workers would have been lost, together with their hard-earned knowledge, and many subcontractors would have had to find other business. Instead, the Air Force stretched out the production of the eleven aircraft already authorized (together with the five for which long-lead items had been approved), so that the Air Force would buy only

The B-2's unveiling provided few clues as to the internal arrangement of its components or to the rationale behind its more unusual features. The dorsal hummock was widely assumed to contain the weapon bay, for example, and yet the bays fit entirely within the wing profile. The strange shape of the leading edge was also apparent, but could not be explained publicly for another decade. *Bill Sweetman*

two or three B-2s per year until the start of full-rate production was authorized.

This also delayed the delivery of test aircraft. The long gap between AV-1 and AV-2 reflected the fact that Northrop had concentrated its efforts on getting AV-1 in the air to validate the bomber's flight performance and to prepare for the RCS tests, because until that could be done there would be no go-ahead for production. The company was reluctant to increase its workforce to build the development aircraft and then end up with more people than were needed for low-rate production, so work on AV-2 and subsequent aircraft slowed down. Northrop and the Air Force stretched out the test program so that it would be finished in June 1997. The last items to be tested were the

defensive management subsystem and some radar modes, because these depended on the navigation and flight control system and could not be validated until those were mature.

But the Air Force, still under heavy fire from the media and Congress, was justifiably concerned about what might happen if it were revealed that the new bomber was still seven to eight years away from a full operational capability—even though the bulk of the delay could be attributed directly to Les Aspin and the House Armed Services Committee. The initial operating capability date for the bomber remained secret.

The mass media, which had largely ignored the B-2 during its years of secret development, was overwhelmingly negative in its coverage of the bomber in 1989 and 1990. Influential outlets such as *Newsweek* and the high-rated TV magazine *60 Minutes* ran damning anti-B-2 diatribes, long on hyperbole, short on evidence, and entirely free of balance. The *60 Minutes* report claimed that "new information," supposedly obtained by a freelance writer named Michael Dennis, showed that the B-2 program would cost $110 billion to $120 billion, not $70 billion as the U.S. Air Force had told Congress. "And what you're saying is that Congress was being lied to by the Air Force to the tune of $40 to $50 billion dollars?" asked *60 Minutes* reporter Mike Wallace. "I believe that's correct," said Dennis. Not one shred of evidence was presented to back up this allegation of criminal misconduct and none has appeared since. The General Accounting Office—no friend of the military—

A guard gives scale to what is in fact a large aircraft. Before the roll-out, it had been widely assumed that the B-2 would be a smaller, lighter aircraft than the B-1, but in fact the Northrop bomber has a greater range and payload. The B-2's wheel track is unusually large, but its short wheelbase makes it compatible with tight turns and relatively narrow taxiways. *Northrop*

Bruce Hinds, chief test pilot for the B-2 program, and Air Force test pilot Colonel Rick Couch were the crew for the B-2's first flight. Once major work on the bomber was complete, a number of minor problems delayed the first flight for several weeks. *Northrop*

found no sign of such an overrun in its report on the B-2, issued a few days later. But Dennis' statement went unchallenged on the air.

Flying-wing critics from the 1940s emerged from holes in the woodwork and were reverently quoted in major newspapers, even though their studies were based on assumptions that did not apply to the B-2. Former Northrop employees alleged that there were safety-of-flight problems with the bomber. They were also widely quoted, and the media seldom explained that they were allied with attorneys bringing ac-

tions under the Civil War–era False Claims Act, under which the whistle-blowers and their lawyers stood to make fortunes if claims were upheld or settled. Again, no evidence has emerged since to indicate that their allegations had any grounding in truth.

Combined with congressional foot-dragging, the media's assault on the B-2 put Northrop and the Air Force on the defensive. In June 1990, in an attempt to dispel some of the myths surrounding the bomber, the Air Force held a B-2 media briefing at Palmdale and described the B-2 and its planned missions in unprecedented detail. The *Wall Street Journal's* reporter summed up the Air Force's entire case in one word: "tendentious." In the same report, he quoted Congressman John Kasich, an opponent of the B-2, as saying that the B-2 would "bankrupt America." Considering that the program's peak annual cost at the time was 1 percent of the defense budget, that statement could (and should) have been called something more than tendentious. It was sheer unadulterated nonsense.

AV-1 went into a lay-up period in the late summer of 1990 and resumed flying in November to carry out initial RCS measurements. Details of the process are still classified, but the tests were carried out incrementally, with components being adjusted and individual "hot-spots" being treated between flights until the desired RCS was attained.

Some of the tests involved flights against ground-based radars, while other tests were performed on the ground, with radars that moved on tracks to image parts of the aircraft. For air-to-air measurements—the only opportunity to examine the aircraft with its wheels up, its engines running, and with no interference from the ground—Northrop used an NTA-3B Skywarrior bomber modified by Metratek to carry its Model 100 AIRSAR radar, in a bizarre frying pan–shaped radome on the rear fuselage.

In 1989, Northrop commissioned a 40 percent scale RCS model from Scaled Composites, the Mojave, California, company founded by Burt Rutan, designer of the Voyager round-the-world aircraft. The 70-foot-span, 6,700-pound model had a carbonfibre-epoxy/foam sandwich structure and was fitted with Northrop-developed RAM edges. The reason why the model was built remains classified, and in a 1998 interview, the U.S. Air Force program office could not even identify it. In 1989, however, Northrop may already have been concerned that the results of stealth testing might not be positive. According to an October 1991 report in the *Wall Street Journal*, Northrop was surprised that summer when Congress imposed RCS testing as a precondition for a production go-ahead. The model may have been used to test alternate RAM systems in case the basic B-2 approach did not work.

There were two significant differences between the B-2 and the F-117, the only stealth aircraft to have passed through full-scale development before it. First, it was much bigger, and it was too large to test on an RCS range at anything like full scale. The largest B-2 model that could be tested was about one-third of full size, whereas Lockheed had tested the F-117 at 70 percent scale. The B-2 was also designed for stealth across a wider range of aspects and frequencies than the F-117. In

AV-1 prepares for its first takeoff on July 17, 1989. Originally, the control surfaces were permitted to droop when the aircraft was at rest, assuming flight positions as it accelerated through 40 to 50 knots. Later, the control laws were changed so that the surfaces normally rest in a streamlined position. *Northrop*

Control surfaces start to come up as AV-1 accelerates for the B-2's maiden flight. Auxiliary inlets are opened whenever the gear is down and the engines are running. A small auxiliary power unit exhaust is open, just behind the inlet. *Northrop*

particular, its leading edges were required to attenuate VHF frequencies—used by the Soviet Tall King early-warning radar—more efficiently than those of the F-117.

These differences were at the root of the problems encountered in RCS testing. Higher-than-predicted reflections were found very early on, and by the summer it was clear that simple adjustments were not enough. The media and Congress panicked, and Air Force Secretary Donald Rice issued elaborate statements to quell the crowd without betraying any significant information.

Fully cleaned up, AV-1 is close to flying speed. Even at high gross weights, the B-2 requires only a modest amount of runway because of its great wing area. The bomber was designed so that it could operate from any of hundreds of U.S. runways that could accommodate a Boeing 727. *Northrop*

Rotation takes place with a barely visible deflection of the bomber's large elevon surfaces. The brake-rudders are cracked open a few degrees because there is a layer of turbulent air above and below the wing. Until the rudders are extended outside that layer, they produce very little drag. By keeping the rudders partly extended, the control system ensures that the controls are effective as soon as they move. *Northrop*

Behind the scenes, the Pentagon's Defense Science Board reviewed the problems. Although details are classified, most observers believe that the problems were encountered in the VHF realm, where stealth is hardest to achieve, and that they were attributable to problems such as gaps, surface discontinuities, and creeping waves, which are very difficult to model or predict and cannot be adequately tested on a scale model.

An early conclusion was that the problems could be solved by changing coatings and edge materials. There was no need to alter the basic structure of the aircraft, so that any solution to the problem could be retrofittable, and B-2 production could be continued. The DSB also noted that, with the break-up of the Soviet Union, it

might make sense to relax the RCS specification in some respects, to reflect threats that the bomber was likely to face, rather than to spend far more money to meet the original requirement.

It was announced in early 1993 that Northrop and Boeing—assisted by Lockheed, which had been summoned to help fix the problem—had developed a set of RCS improvements that would be applied to the last B-2s off the line and retrofitted to earlier aircraft. This fix was described as the least costly and least risky of three options that had been studied.

Stealth performance parameters are, naturally, classified; however, the Block 30 aircraft, with the final signature modifications, should have an RCS that is at least two to three orders of magnitude less than the kind of conventional

The B-2 lifts off smoothly. The landing gear remained extended for the 2-hour, 20-minute first flight, which concluded at Edwards Air Force Base in California.
Northrop

target that radars are designed to detect. The effect is to reduce the radar's range by a factor of four to eight. The radars are less effective, and their areas of coverage no longer overlap: with mission planning and the defensive management subsystem, the bomber can weave between them. It is worth noting that the F-117, with a not-dissimilar RCS to the B-2 and no real-time data on hostile radars, was able to raid Baghdad and survive even though the Iraqi defense forces had good reason to guess when and where the fighters would attack.

Even when the RCS problems appeared, the Air Force maintained that the B-2 was stealthier than the F-117, with an equal or better RCS over a larger bandwidth. Northrop Grumman

engineers have claimed that the B-2 is "the most survivable aircraft in existence." And, although a senior Lockheed Martin engineer has privately disputed Northrop's claim, he was not talking about the F-117, but the Mach 3 SR-71.

Claimed "detections" of B-2s making air show appearances should be taken with more than a pinch of salt. The F-117 is equipped with means to increase its RCS at will, for two good reasons: to ensure that civilian ATC can see the aircraft in a "skin paint" mode and to prevent any unauthorized radar operator from acquiring real RCS data. The B-2 indubitably has the same capability and uses it routinely. As for British Aerospace's much-touted imaging of a B-2 at a few kilometers' range at Farnborough in 1996:

One of the first tasks in the flight-test program was to open the flight-refueling envelope. Refueling behind the KC-135 is a challenge. On other large airplanes, the refueling receptacle is well ahead of the wing—on the B-2, it is on the wing quarter-chord line, so the entire wing is close behind the tanker. The two aircraft interact strongly: the B-2's "bow wave" pushes up on the tanker's stabilizer, and the B-2's big, lightly loaded wing is in the slipstream from the tanker's wing and engines. *Northrop*

how often will a defender see the top of a B-2, and how useful is it to see an aircraft at 3 miles (5 kilometers) when it flies 9 miles (15 kilometers) high—or more—and can deliver a conventional bomb from 13 nautical miles (25 kilometers)?

Meanwhile, the remaining test aircraft had joined the program. AV-3, flying in June 1991,

was the first radar and navigation test aircraft. It was equipped with the APQ-181 in 1993. AV-4 and AV-5, designated for avionics and weapons testing, followed in April and October 1992, and the last development aircraft, AV-6, flew in February 1993. AV-4 dropped the first weapon in the test program, an inert 2,000-

pound Mk84 bomb, in September 1993. The NKC-135A avionics test bed resumed flying in 1992 to support tests of the TF/TA radar modes. In early 1993, after 352 hours, AV-1 was placed in storage. With its incomplete avionics suite and nonstandard instrumentation, it could no longer contribute to the program.

The first production B-2, AV-1007, was completed in August 1993 but leased back to Northrop for electromagnetic compatibility testing. The second, AV-1008, was delivered to

Refueling from the KC-10 is much easier. Twice the weight of the KC-135, the KC-10 is naturally less susceptible to "surfing" on the bomber's bow wave, and the refueling boom is much longer. Together with the KC-10's greater length, this keeps the bomber away from the core of the tanker's wake. *Northrop*

Whiteman Air Force Base, Missouri, in December 1993. The Air Force announced that the bomber would be named Spirit and that each B-2 would be named after a U.S. state. But this reflected a hard fact: the 50 states would provide plenty of names for the B-2 force, because the program was scaled back to near extinction.

The backdrop to Washington battles over the B-2 was the collapse of the Soviet Union. By 1990, with the Soviet Union on the verge of breaking up, the Democrat-controlled Congress was pressing the Bush administration for cuts in defense expenditures (the so-called "peace dividend"). The B-2 was a prime target, but the larger concern was that several large aircraft programs—the B-2, the Navy's A-12 attack aircraft, the Air Force's Advanced Tactical Fighter, and the C-17 transport—were expected to be in full-rate production by the mid-1990s, and they could not all be supported by lower budgets.

A compromise was announced in April 1990, when Defense Secretary Richard Cheney unveiled the results of the Pentagon's Major Aircraft Review (MAR). The MAR kept all the Pentagon's aircraft projects alive but sharply reduced production numbers in the mid-1990s. Under the MAR, the total planned B-2 buy was cut from 132 to 75 aircraft, and the production rate was cut drastically. Instead of a steady increase to a maximum of 33 aircraft in the final year, the rate would reach a plateau of 12 aircraft a year in the mid-1990s. Then-year program cost would decline from $75.4 billion (having increased since late 1988 due to the delay in production) to $61.1 billion.

Ironically, one of the programs preserved by the MAR, largely at the B-2's expense, was the Navy's A-12. Cheney and Congress were equally unaware that the A-12 was in grave trouble, because the Navy was concealing the problems that had resulted from the arrogance and ineptitude of the service's top commanders and civilian leaders. Nine months later, the program was dead.

Politically, the MAR cutbacks did not secure the future of the B-2, but made it more precarious. It was a matter of economics. Overall, the MAR had accomplished a 19 percent cost savings as a result of a 43 percent cut in output. This may seem asymmetric, but it has to be remembered that the nonrecurring costs of the program were unaffected by the cutback (most of them had been spent) and savings were further offset by the lower and less efficient production rate. When production is cut, it is always the cheapest aircraft that are cut first, but the MAR numbers allowed B-2 foes to talk about "the $850 million" B-2.

The B-2 would henceforth be dogged by the fiscal fiction of the "then-year unit program cost": the total cost of the program, including inflation to the date of its completion, divided by the number of aircraft built. This may be a useful number in comparing options at the start of a program, but loses meaning as the project progresses. By 1990, for the B-2, it was irrelevant. You could not save $850 million for every B-2 cancelled, and an extra B-2 would not cost $850 million. Nevertheless, it was the only figure that the media would use.

In October 1991, Congress froze production at 16 aircraft, in the aftermath of the summer's failed military coup in the Soviet Union, the irreversible break-up of the Warsaw Pact, and the bad news from the RCS tests. In an attempt to turn the apparently inevitable halting of the program into a political asset in an election

year, President Bush announced in January 1992 that the administration would seek funds for only 5 more B-2s, bringing production to 21, including the 6 test aircraft.

The cutback was one of a group of post–Cold War changes to the U.S. strategic forces, which included a fundamental restructuring of the U.S. Air Force. In June 1992, the Strategic Air Command ceased to exist, and the Air Force's heavy bombers were reassigned to the newly formed Air Combat Command (ACC).

The last significant event of 1992, for the B-2 program, was the presidential election. The incoming Democratic administration, accompanied by a new and largely liberal influx of representatives and senators, was hardly likely to authorize an increase in the number of B-2s. This was confirmed by the appointment of Les Aspin as secretary of defense. As the former chair of the House Armed Services Committee, Aspin was instrumental in delaying and cutting back the B-2 program.

An important tool in the development of the B-2 was the NKC-135A Flight Test Avionics Laboratory (FTAL) equipped with elements of the B-2's radar, navigation system, computers, and cockpit displays. By the time the B-2 made its first flight, the FTAL was already running as much software as a complete B-1. Northrop

The reasons why this 40 percent scale RCS model of the B-2 was commissioned from Scaled Composites and tested in 1989 remain classified. It was delivered to Northrop's RCS range in Tejon, California, where it was fitted with Northrop-developed edge materials and coatings. *Scaled Composites*

Hopes that more B-2s might be produced rose in November 1994, when the Republican party unexpectedly seized control of the House and Senate. In May 1995, the House added $500 million to the FY 1996 defense budget to start producing two more B-2s, and Northrop Grumman (Northrop had acquired Grumman in 1994) offered to build 20 more aircraft at a flyaway cost of $566 million each.

The logic behind the proposal was solid. The 1993 Bottom-Up Review of the U.S. military

Cold-weather tests of the B-2 were conducted at Eielson Air Force Base, Alaska, in March 1993, confirming the results of 1993 tests in the Air Force's giant "cold chamber" at Eglin Air Force Base, Florida. *Northrop*

posture had confirmed the need for long-range bombers, because of their unique ability to bring heavy firepower to bear anywhere in the world at short notice, and supported the retention of the B-52H, B-1, and B-2. Building more B-2s, at a slow rate, would keep the force effective, despite attrition, and in the longer term provide a replacement for the B-52.

The action was supported by the Senate, but opposed by the administration and the Air Force, and the money was earmarked instead to bring AV-1 to operational status and to fund other improvements. Ultimately, the Clinton administration's opposition to the B-2 was and is political. The cutbacks in production have driven the "then-year unit program cost" of the B-2 above $2 billion dollars. This number is based on dividing the total cost of the program by the number of aircraft built and is a fiscal fiction. Nevertheless, braying politicians and know-nothing columnists have now lodged the number in the public mind, to the point where few people will advocate building more B-2s.

Generally, too, the Clinton administration has been content to defer major military modernization costs until after 2000, keeping the current budgets balanced and leaving later administrations to pay the bills. This pattern is also visible in fighter modernization.

The Air Force's opposition to more B-2s is pragmatic: The service considers that the money would be better spent elsewhere. The B-2 is a valuable aircraft, but it is not cheap to acquire or to operate, and the Air Force's tactical forces have already been substantially cut back. The demise of SAC did not favor the B-2; while ACC has not ignored bomber modernization, the new command is inevitably dominated by fighter pilots who are reluctant to see more fighter

AV-5 approaches Eielson for cold-weather trials. Are we looking at the bottom or top of this aircraft? Frankly, it is impossible to tell. *Northrop*

wings shut down in order to fund small numbers of bombers.

A bomber study, announced by the Pentagon in May 1995, showed that bombers were important in the first stages of a regional war—the so-called "halt phase"—but that forward-based tactical aircraft were increasingly important as the conflict continued. Overall, therefore, investing more money in bombers was not worthwhile if it drew money away from tactical aircraft. Within the bomber force, the study showed, investment in new conventional weapons and improvements for the B-1B

The B-2 rests in a light snowfall at Eielson. This aircraft, AV-5, was later named *Spirit of Ohio* and will be delivered as a full operational B-2 Block 30 in early 2000.

had a greater pay-off than the construction of new B-2s.

All studies depend on the assumptions, however. The 1995 study, for example, used a zero-sum model bounded by an already constrained Air Force budget. That is, any money spent on the B-2 had to be pulled out of other Air Force spending in the same year. It did not compare the effectiveness of more B-2s with the cost and value of carrier-based strike aircraft, which also constitute a quick-reaction asset, available before Air Force tactical air power arrives in the theater. Providing the U.S. Navy with a long-range, stealthy strike aircraft, a version of the Joint Strike Fighter, will be a large investment in the early 2000s. Neither did the Air Force study consider restrictions on in-theater bases, whether due to indecisive or weak allies or to enemy action.

Another argument with some merit is that the B-52H, armed with the new Lockheed Martin AGM-158 Joint Air-to-Surface Standoff Missile (JASSM), will be useful until 2015 to 2020; and by that time a replacement long-range aircraft may be very different from the B-2. A future bomber might not need the same payload as the B-2, particularly with today's smaller, more accurate weapons. Unrefueled range could be traded off against tanker support: There is no need

As the test program continued, AV-2 was placed in flyable storage. Here it is seen with AV-1 (left) at Palmdale in 1991.
Northrop

for a 1,000-nautical mile (1,800-kilometer) penetration of hostile territory if the Soviet Union is not the target. A new bomber would take advantage of the more modern stealth technology developed for the F-22 and Joint Strike Fighter, and it would certainly use less costly avionics. Despite the development bill, it might be cheaper in the long run than more B-2s.

Indeed, it is not impossible that such an aircraft already exists or could be available quickly. From the early days of the B-2 program, Northrop was studying scaled-down versions of the design, including a carrier-based aircraft. The Navy was impressed and developed the Advanced Tactical Aircraft (ATA) requirement. From the few leaked reports that described it, this appeared to be a replacement for the A-6. While this was partly true, the ATA was a more ambitious project with a much greater range and war load than any previous Navy bomber, and was designed to attack the Soviet Navy's bases around the North Cape.

Northrop and Grumman teamed for the ATA contract, producing a design that was almost an exact 40 percent scale model of the original B-2 design, before the low-level modifications. They were pitted against a McDonnell Douglas/General Dynamics team in a competitive demonstration-validation program, which started in November 1984. In the final source

The Block 30 modernization process starts with the removal of the B-2's external coatings. In search of a nontoxic stripping medium that would not damage the bomber's skin, Northrop Grumman developed a system using crystallized wheat starch and compressed air. The sharp-edged crystals break up the coatings into a dry residue that can be easily cleaned up. *Northrop*

selection, the Navy insisted on a fixed-price bid for research and development. Northrop refused to comply with this directive, and its rivals were awarded the contract to develop the A-12 Avenger II. Suffering from poor management and excessive weight growth, the Avenger II was cancelled at the beginning of 1991.

Nonetheless, an aircraft similar in shape and size to the Northrop Grumman ATA was seen on at least two occasions in 1993–1994, suggesting that the U.S. Air Force, which was supposed to buy the A-12 as an F-111 replacement but had been skeptical about the developers' lack of stealth experience, may have secretly sponsored flight-testing of the B-2-based design. With an unrefueled combat radius of 700 to 900 nautical miles, and a 10,000-pound internal weapon load, such an aircraft would have a significantly greater range and war load than any contemporary tactical aircraft.

Whatever the answer, during the course of 1996 to 1997, it became clear that no more B-2s would be built. The cost of doing so increases day by day, as suppliers wind up their production lines and as experienced workers move to other jobs. The Palmdale plant remains busy, however, because a good deal of work is still to be done on the 21-aircraft program.

While the B-2 debate drew to a close, testing proceeded on a deliberate, complex schedule, with aircraft being grounded periodically so that they could be upgraded with new hardware and software for the next series of flights. Avionics hardware and software paced the schedule, but the program office noted in late 1996 that development had broadly followed the schedule laid down in 1989. While not every radar and defensive management subsystem mode was available for testing on time, many of the modes were

Working from platforms suspended from the ceiling of the B-2 paint hangar, workers wear protective suits and breathe filtered air as they remove classified and sometimes toxic coating materials from the bomber's surface. The panels at lower right protect specialized and expensive communications antennas from damage. *Northrop*

emerged during flight testing: structural cracking in the aft decks and problems with the radomes. A new aft deck material (unspecified, but possibly based on carbon-carbon composites) was developed for retrofit to the aircraft and incorporated from the 14th aircraft. The original plastic radomes were found to absorb water, degrading the performance of the radar, and have been replaced by a honeycomb material.

The only other major shortfall in the system's performance is the defensive management subsystem. Despite a $740 million investment, the defensive management subsystem (DMS) has not been developed to the point where it meets the original requirement. In particular, the system's ability to locate and identify "pop-up" threats is not what it was intended to be. In operational testing in late 1997, the system provided inaccurate or cluttered information and produced excessive workloads for its operators.

The basic B-2 test program was completed on July 1, 1997. Originally, in 1986, the Air Force planned a four-year, 3,600-hour program. In fact, the effort took eight years and 5,000 hours. Much of the extra time on the calendar reflected delays in production. Added flights and hours addressed unexpected problems, the need to test fixes to the exhaust and leading edges, and changes to the bomber's mission and weapons.

Because of the production delays imposed by Congress, it was clear that more than three years would elapse between the delivery of the first production aircraft, AV-1007, and the completion of flight testing. The Air Force and Northrop accordingly laid out a three-stage plan that synchronized deliveries, flight-testing, and the working-up of the operational wing at Whiteman.

not dependent on others, so another part of the test program could be brought forward to use the aircraft and other resources. As a result, some modes were delivered ahead of schedule and the entire program remained on track.

Apart from the RCS problem and the anticipated detail headaches with radar performance, only two substantial airframe-related problems

The plan defined three B-2 configurations, or Blocks. To ease the type's entry into service, two principles were adopted: the operational unit would always have at least eight aircraft in a common configuration, and there would never be more than two versions in the field at the same time.

The first 10 production B-2s—AV-1007 through AV-1016—were delivered as Block 10 (B-2A-10-NO) aircraft between December 1993 and the end of 1995. The Block 10's primary role was as a trainer for pilots and maintenance crews. It did not operate at full flight loads (being limited to a maximum takeoff weight of 305,000 pounds/138,300 kilograms), had no terrain-following or precision-weapons capability, and had a limited capability in the Defensive Management System (DMS). The last Block 10 aircraft was withdrawn from service in early 1997.

The Block 20 (B-2A-20-NO) was the first operational variant and was described as "contributing to the integrated air campaign" because it is armed with the GATS/GAM precision strike weapon. It operates up to a peacetime takeoff weight of 336,500 pounds (152,600 kilograms). It is cleared for manual terrain-following down to 600 feet, and the DMS is operational in Bands 1–3. The Block 20 also introduced an improved environmental control system.

Three new Block 20 aircraft (1017–1019) were delivered in 1996, the last arriving in August. Starting in mid-1996, the five newest Block 10s (1012–1016) went through a 12- to 16-week modification program to bring them up to Block 20 status. With the arrival of the fifth modified aircraft in May 1997, the 509th had eight Block 20s on strength. The B-2 had been declared operational for conventional strike missions in January 1997, and after passing standard nuclear certification tests, the 509th attained initial operating capability in April 1997.

The definitive B-2 configuration is the Block 30 (B-2A-30-NO). The first two Block 30s were AV-1020 and 1021, the last two B-2s and the only B-2s to be delivered off the production line in this form. They arrived at Whiteman in late 1997, along with AV-1008, the first aircraft to be upgraded. By late 1998, eight Block 30s were in service and six more were due to be delivered during 1999, leading to a full operational capability late in 1999. The scale of the Block 30 modifications can be gauged from the fact that the first modifications took two years; even the Block 20s are on the ground for a year when they are modified.

The Block 30 modification includes the removal and replacement of all the aircraft's edges, including the leading edges and control surfaces, in order to meet RCS requirements. The leading edges, visibly segmented on the Block 20, will be joined into an electrically continuous structure. Aircraft prior to AV-1014 receive the new aft deck structure.

All the surface coatings on the B-2, including absorbent and conductive layers, are removed and replaced with improved materials. After having a great deal of difficulty in finding an environmentally safe stripping medium that would remove the coatings without damaging the composite skins, Northrop Grumman developed a technique to "depaint" the B-2 using crystallized wheat starch and high-pressure air.

The modification includes some rewiring, particularly for the test aircraft. New weapons

include JDAM, and the Bomb Rack Assembly units are being used for the first time, allowing the B-2 to carry CBU-87s, mines, or other small stores.

Avionics software and hardware changes include automatic TF/TA down to 200 feet and the installation of a Milstar satellite communications terminal. DMS reaches its full capability with the addition of Band 4, allowing crews to replan their missions in flight when an unexpected threat is detected. Although the system does not meet original requirements, the Air Force is developing improvements that allow the DMS to work better. The changes are introduced as part of the continuous improvement of the B-2's software and meet "the basic needs of the user," according to the program office. One saving factor is that any likely threat today will be less dense and less deep than the Soviet air defense system against which the DMS was designed.

Another change, introduced in two phases in Blocks 20 and 30, is the integration of the B-2 with the Air Force Mission Support System (AFMSS). This replaces the Strategic Mission Development and Planning System (SMDPS), which was originally developed for the B-2. The SMDPS was designed for nuclear warfighting and was never intended to be installed outside the B-2's main operating bases. The switch to the transportable AFMSS will allow the B-2 to sustain operations from bases around the world and makes it easier to integrate the B-2 with other Air Force operations.

Early versions of the AFMSS software were unsatisfactory, and operators found that it took longer than expected to plan B-2 missions; but a new release of the program in late 1998 has improved its performance, and its operators have also learned to use it more efficiently. In April 1999, the system was due to be upgraded again, with the addition of the Common Low Observable Auto-Router (CLOAR). This is a software package, used on the AFMSS to support the B-2, F-117, and future stealth aircraft, which develops a mission plan that shows the stealth aircraft's least visible aspects to known threats.

While the B-2's development has taken a long time, it should be remembered that the aircraft is unique. It has carried a generation of stealth development on its shoulders, as other programs have slipped or been canceled. It has also undergone a complete change in its primary mission, from a nuclear bomber that flies alone to a conventional strike aircraft, cooperating with other forces and carrying a unique range of ordnance.

AV-14, *Spirit of Georgia*, was one of the last B-2s to be delivered as a Block 10, in May 1995. The aircraft returned to service as a Block 20 in 1997 and was due to complete its Block 30 modernization in September 1999. *Northrop*

WEAPONS FOR A NEW MISSION

As the B-2 has matured, it has been cleared to use a wide variety of weapons. The B-2 is one of the most versatile combat aircraft in the world in terms of weapon carriage, with a 50,000-pound (22,700-kilogram) maximum load divided between two generously sized weapon bays. Each bay accommodates either a Boeing-developed advanced rotary launcher (ARL) capable of carrying eight 2,000-pound class weapons or a bomb rack assembly (BRA) unit for carrying smaller conventional weapons. The maximum load of 80 Mk82 500-pound bombs was first released in March 1998 by a B-2 operating from Guam.

The B-2 was designed for nuclear strike and is still assigned to that mission. Its principal weapon in this role would be the B83 nuclear bomb. The B83 is the newest type of strategic nuclear bomb developed for the Air Force and was designed by the Department of Energy's Lawrence Livermore National Laboratory in California. It has a selectable yield between one and two megatons and is the first production bomb to be designed for "laydown" delivery against hard, irregular targets. In such a delivery, the bomb is delay-fused so that the bomber can escape to a safe distance before the explosion. In contrast to airburst or contact fusing, however, this means that the bomb must survive the initial impact with the ground and land without bouncing or rolling.

The B-2 can also carry the B61-11 penetrating nuclear weapon. First test-dropped from the B-2 in March 1998, the B61-11 is the first new U.S. nuclear weapon to be designed since production of new warheads was suspended in 1989 and is produced by modifying existing B61-7 bombs. It was designed because of concerns that potential adversaries, such as Libya, were acquiring large stocks of tunneling

AV-4, weapons workhorse of the B-2 fleet, releases multiple Mk82 500-pound bombs in an August 1995 mission. The B-2 can carry 80 such weapons. *Northrop*

A B-2 releases a B83 thermonuclear weapon test shape. The bomb's drogue chute has opened immediately after release, and the main parachute—packed to the density of an oak log—is already pulled clear and is starting to open. The aim here is a "soft lay-down" delivery from low altitude, which requires the parachute to open as quickly as possible. *U.S. Air Force*

equipment and might be attempting to conceal nuclear and chemical weapon stocks in tunnel complexes under hard rock. The U.S. Air Force retained a few multimegaton B53 weapons to deal with such targets, but only the relatively vulnerable B-52 can carry them. The B61-11 was produced by Sandia National Laboratory and combines the B61-7 warhead with a selectable yield ranging from 10 kilotons to 340 kilotons, with a new hardened-steel, needle-nosed casing. It has no parachute and added stabilizing fins. The weapon will penetrate 15 to 25 feet into the ground, transferring a much

greater part of its energy into ground shock.

A third nuclear weapon was designed for the B-2, but later canceled. The Boeing AGM-131A SRAM II (Short-Range Attack Missile) was a direct replacement for the original Boeing AGM-69 SRAM, which was produced in the 1960s. It consisted of a 200-kiloton warhead, a rocket motor, and a Litton laser-gyro inertial navigation system. The SRAM II was due to enter service in 1993, but its development was terminated as part of the nuclear weapons cutbacks ordered by President Bush in September 1991. Physically, the B-2's weapon bay can accommodate Boeing's AGM-86 Air-Launched Cruise Missile (ALCM) or AGM-129 Advanced Cruise Missile (ACM). Although these weapons were not originally intended for the B-2, Pentagon planners apparently considered that improving Soviet defenses might force the B-2 to use "shoot and penetrate" tactics, in which the bomber carries a mix of high-yield bombs and cruise missiles. The cruise missiles act as armed decoys (a concept which was actually the genesis of the cruise missile concept), forcing the defenders to deal with more weapons. Air Combat Command documents mention plans for integrating the AGM-86C Conventional ALCM (CALCM) on the B-2, but there is no firm date for such an effort.

After the fall of the Soviet Union, the B-2's conventional capability came to the fore, as did a glaring anomaly: the world's most advanced military aircraft, with a highly accurate and expensive targeting system, had no precision weapon. Existing guided bombs, too, were unsuitable for the B-2: laser-guided weapons were not effective from the B-2's operating altitude, and TV-guided bombs required a datalink that was hard to reconcile with stealth. The B-2's need for an accurate weapon has now been

Prototype B83 in the National Atomic Museum. The B83 was designed at the Livermore National Laboratory in California as a less costly substitute for the B77, which had been canceled. The B83 has a selectable yield between 1 and 2 megatons. *Bill Sweetman*

filled by a new, very different class of weapon, which approaches the precision of a laser-guided bomb but is fully autonomous and costs one-fifth as much.

The concept was simple: fit an inertial measurement unit (IMU) in a bomb tail with moving fins, and, just before release, program the weapon with the flight path that the aircraft's weapon control system predicts that it will follow to the target. The guidance system will then take out random errors (such as those caused as the bomb wobbles through the aircraft's flow field) and unpredictable factors, such as changes in wind speed and direction. A number of companies, including Northrop, worked under U.S.

Air Force research contracts in the later 1980s to develop this class of weapon and to reduce the cost of the guidance system.

After the Gulf War, in which Coalition aircraft were forced to bomb from unexpectedly high altitudes, this concept was refined with the addition of a global positioning system (GPS) receiver, and became the basis of a high-priority, large-scale program: the Joint Direct Attack Munition (JDAM). Because this weapon would not be available until late in the decade, however, Northrop Grumman proposed a quick-reaction program to build a small number of similar weapons for the B-2 force and to integrate a GPS receiver on the aircraft.

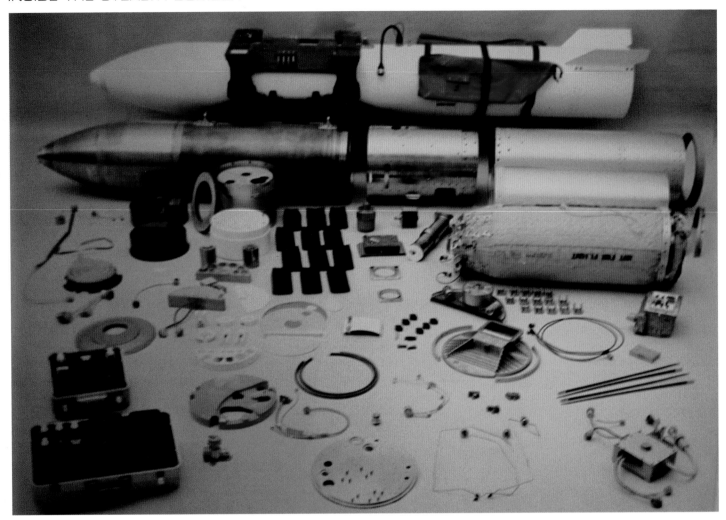

The B83 is a complex system. The parachute occupies the rear portion of the case, which accommodates the warhead itself and an elaborate safing and arming system. *U.S. Air Force*

This system is known as GPS Aided Targeting System/GPS Aided Munition (GATS/GAM). GATS is designed to reduce the target location error of the B-2's bombing systems. Although the B-2's radar is capable of very high resolution, it includes inherent errors—such as INS error, uncertainty in the relative altitude of the target and the bomber, and Doppler error—which prevent the system from computing the exact distance from the aircraft to the target. This remaining zone of uncertainty is the target location error.

GATS uses GPS to correct for inertial error. In a GATS attack, the bomber makes a dog-leg approach to the target, taking several radar shots at the target and another fixed point from positions at least 30 degrees apart. This changes the relationship among the components of the target location error, allowing system software to estimate Doppler and altitude errors. The result is that GATS/GAM meets a circular error probability requirement of 20 feet (6 meters) (at least half the weapons will fall within 6 meters of the target), compared with a 40-foot (13 meters) circular error probability requirement for the standard JDAM. All 16 weapons can be released against different targets in a single pass. Alternatively, multiple weapons can be aimed at one target: The weapon is maneuverable enough to allow several weapons launched in sequence to strike the same target from their different release points.

The GAM bomb is designated GBU-36/B. It is a 2,000-pound (900-kilogram) Mk84 bomb with a readily installed tail-kit and a significant stand-off range. From a 40,000-foot Mach 0.8 release, the weapon can glide more than 13 nautical miles (25 kilometers) downrange, or 8 nautical miles (15 kilometers) down range and

Boeing's AGM-131 SRAM II would have been the B-2's primary weapon against relocatable targets such as mobile missile systems. The Mach 4 missile, with an extremely low RCS on its own account, would have had a range of 50 to 200 nautical miles, depending in its launch altitude. Development was canceled in 1992. *Bill Sweetman*

cross-range, and hit its target at a 60-degree impact angle with undiminished accuracy.

An all-up demonstration of GATS/GAM took place in October 1996. Three B-2s launched from Whiteman and dropped 16 live GAMs on 16 semi-trailers located on the Nellis Air Force Base range in Nevada. The leading aircraft dropped eight weapons, the rest being shared with the other two. All the targets were hit, and the third bomber used its radar to perform bomb damage assessment, imaging wreckage and the bomb craters.

Comprising an off-the-shelf warhead with a new hardened case, the B61-11 is designed to penetrate into the ground before exploding. Even a relatively shallow penetration greatly increases the weapon's effectiveness against hardened and buried targets. *James C. Goodall*

The basic GBU-36/B has now been replaced by the U.S. Air Force standard Joint Direct Attack Munition (JDAM). McDonnell Douglas (now Boeing) was selected to develop and produce JDAM in October 1995, and the weapon achieved early operational capability on the B-2 Block 30 in July 1997. As far as the B-2 is concerned, its significance is that it can be used with the BLU-109 hard-target munition, allowing the B-2 to attack deeply buried or fortified targets.

The Pentagon plans to acquire 87,000 JDAM guidance kits. The overall aim is to provide enough JDAMs to meet the needs of any future conflict without resorting to heavy unguided weapons. JDAM comprises a new tail with movable fins, containing a Honeywell ring-laser-gyro inertial measurement unit, a Lockheed Martin (Loral) computer, a Rockwell Collins GPS receiver, and an HR Textron actua-

tor system. The weapon is powered by a thermal battery. Mated to a 2,000-pound (900-kilogram) warhead, either a Mk84 blast/fragmentation type or a BLU-109, the weapon is designated GBU-31.

A key test of JDAM took place in April 1998, when a B-2 released four BLU-109-armed JDAMs against three targets on the White Sands Missile Range in New Mexico. Two weapons were dropped on the same point, hitting the target so accurately that the second weapon entered the cavity formed by the first—a standard of accuracy previously attainable only at close range with laser or TV guidance. According to the Air Force, the damage caused by the sequential blasts was greater than predicted.

From the outset, JDAM has been designed to be mated with a nose-mounted seeker for greater accuracy. Under current plans, a demonstration/validation program for the seeker will start in 2002, which implies serious study of cost and performance issues from 2000 onward. The Air Force is also looking at an extended-range JDAM with folding wings, and a 500-pound (225 kilogram) inertially guided weapon. The B-2 could carry and launch 76 of these.

As JDAM enters service, the remaining GAM tail-kits are being mated with the BLU-113 hard-target warhead. Designed to destroy bunkers up to 100 feet deep, the 4,700-pound BLU-113 was developed under a quick-reaction program during Desert Storm, in a thinly veiled attempt to "de-capitate" the Iraqi command by killing Saddam Hussein and his principal commanders. The first bombs were modified from Navy-surplus 203-millimeter gun barrels, fitted with nose and tail caps and mated to Texas Instruments Pave-way III laser-guidance kits. In this form, the bomb was designated GBU-28. Since the retire-ment of the F-111F it has been carried on the F-15E, and the Air Force has acquired at least 100 new munitions from National Forge. A GAM-equipped version of the weapon was test-dropped from a B-2 in early 1997. Provisionally designated GAM-113, it is now identified as the

The 2,000-pound Boeing GBU-31 Joint Direct Attack Munition (JDAM) is the B-2's primary conventional weapon. The JDAM kit comprises a self-contained tail unit and a "jacket" carrying four stabilizing fins. The guidance system consists of a low-cost inertial/GPS unit and movable tailfins and steers the bomb to follow the path predicted by the bomber's weapon-aiming software. *James C. Goodall*

AV-4 releases a JDAM on an early test drop. The bomber can carry 16 JDAMs and, in theory, can release all of them against different targets on a single pass. Alternatively, multiple JDAMs can be aimed at a single point, after being released sequentially at different points in space. Very visible in this view are the retractable wingtip navigation lights. Often seen open in daylight, these probably also serve to augment the bomber's radar return and mask its true RCS. *Northrop*

GBU-37/B. The B-2 can carry eight of these weapons, four on each rotary launcher.

The Air Force is looking at other improvements to the BLU-113, including a hard target smart fuse (HTSF) that can count the layers in an underground structure (as the bomb passes through a void, its deceleration rate changes) and can be programmed to detonate at a certain level. A variant of the weapon with a tungsten-loaded explosive charge, weighing around 7,000 pound (3,200 kilograms), could be used to increase the weapon's mass-to-diameter ratio and hence its penetration depth.

Before leaving the subject of deep-penetration weapons, it might be appropriate to mention the ultimate hard-target weapon, proposed by Lockheed Martin and known as Big BLU. This would be a 22,000 pound (10,000-kilogram) class bomb with a high-density nose section

(filled with depleted uranium or a similarly dense material) and a GPS/inertial guidance system. In early 1997, Big BLU was a candidate for Advanced Concept Technology Demonstrator (ACTD) funds, which would support the building of a small number of weapons for test and contingency operational use.

Also being introduced on the B-2 is the Raytheon AGM-154 Joint Stand-Off Weapon (JSOW). A modular glide weapon, the JSOW is being developed in three versions. The "baseline" AGM-154A carries 154 of the BLU-97 submunitions used in the CBU-87 CEM cluster bomb. Its primary targets are air defense sites and soft-skinned and lightly protected vehicles. The AGM-154B anti-armor version carries 6 BLU-108/B SFW submunitions, with a total of 24 warheads. The Navy will carry the weapon on the F/A-18. Test drops from the B-2 were due

The BLU-113 warhead that is used in the GBU-37/B was developed rapidly during the Gulf War and was not specifically intended for the B-2; however, the bomber's very long weapon bays accommodate the weapon easily. When weapons are being loaded on the B-2, one bay is closed and the inboard door of the other bay swings out and up against the belly, and the weapon bay spoilers are stowed. *Northrop Grumman*

to start in April 1999, and the bomber can carry 16 such weapons.

One weapon intended for the B-2 never saw service. The Northrop AGM-137A Tri-Service Standoff Attack Missile (TSSAM) was a stealthy missile with a 250-nautical mile (450-kilometer) range, an 800-pound (360-kilogram) hard-target penetrator warhead, and an autonomous precision guidance system. After a series of problems and cost overruns, TSSAM was canceled in 1994, leaving the B-2 without a stand-off capability.

There are a number of operational situations where such a capability could be useful. For example, a B-2 armed with stand-off missiles could fly undetected to a launch point inside an adversary's airspace and simultaneously attack 16 high-value point targets that could be as much as 400 nautical miles apart. Alternatively, a B-2 could deliver direct attack weapons on a primary target and launch long-range weapons against other objectives.

After TSSAM, the U.S. Air Force launched a program to develop a lower-cost substitute. The Joint Air-to-Surface Standoff Missile (JASSM) benefits from the expensive lessons learned in TSSAM, combined with improvements in electronic technology and stealth. It was developed with a less stringent set of requirements, however, and under a streamlined management plan. These changes have dramatically reduced its cost.

The JASSM program office defined a basic, operationally related requirement for the new

The B-2's most devastating conventional weapon is the 4,700-pound GBU-37/B hard-target bomb. With its considerable mass and great length-to-diameter ratio, coupled with a GPS/inertial guidance system and a sophisticated fuse, the GBU-37/B can threaten heavily protected, complex bunkers. It uses the guidance systems originally delivered for the Northrop Grumman GPS Aided Munition (GAM). *James C. Goodall*

A GBU-37 drops from AV-4. Qualifying new weapons from the B-2 is relatively easy, because all the stores are carried internally. The weapons have no impact on drag and handling, eliminating a great deal of flight testing. Modern U.S. weapons use a standard interface to transfer data from the aircraft to the weapon's guidance system, simplifying integration. *U.S. Air Force*

missile. The most important of the essential requirements were a minimum range (which is classified, but probably between 160 and 240 nautical miles); the ability to fit on a bomber's rotary launcher, which set a 14-foot length limit; compatibility with the F/A-18, setting a 2,200-pound (1,000-kilogram) limit to its total weight; and a cost ceiling of $700,000.

Boeing and Lockheed Martin took these requirements into a competitive demonstration effort from 1996 to 1998. Provided that the JASSM candidates met the few fundamental requirements, they would be assessed on an effectiveness parameter, defined as the number of missiles required to kill a defined set of 17 targets. This left the competitors free to conduct trades. Do you offer a very stealthy missile that will never be shot down, or a less costly weapon that might be shot down 5 percent of the time? Should some of the missiles have an advanced

seeker, or should all of them have an inexpensive one? Both teams designed and tested hardware, including captive-carry and release tests of prototype missiles. Lockheed Martin was selected as the winner in April 1998.

The AGM-158 JASSM is based on a low-observable airframe shape derived from earlier Skunk Works designs, with a sharply swept folding wing and no horizontal tail. The airframe is composite, but its manufacturing techniques owe more to builders of boats, windmills, and surfboards than to aerospace. The engine is a Teledyne Ryan J402, but with many detail modifications that reduce its cost by 40 percent compared with today's J402. The 1,000-pound (450-kilogram) J-1000 warhead combines penetrating and blast/fragmentation effects.

The missile uses GPS/inertial midcourse guidance and has an imaging infrared terminal seeker. JASSM is an autonomous weapon: The

To reduce the demand on scarce B-2s, the Air Force has built a realistic weapons loading trainer at Whiteman Air Force Base. It represents the bomber's complete lower center-section, including weapon-bay doors, landing gear, and crew access ladder, and can be fitted with either of the B-2's standard weapon carriage systems. Here, the Advanced Rotary Launcher (ARL) is installed. *James C. Goodall*

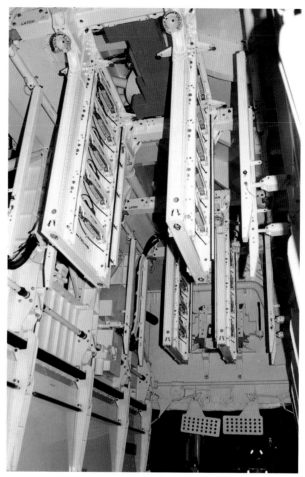

The Bomb Rack Assembly (BRA) is an easily reconfigured system that can carry a wide range of weapons in the 500- to 1,000-pound range. Weapons are attached laterally to the vertical racks. Each BRA can carry 20 500-pound Mk82s or nine Tactical Munitions Dispensers and can be wired for guided weapons. Two racks are installed in each weapon bay. *James C. Goodall*

seeker will be preprogrammed with an image of the target and will automatically guide it to the correct aim point. With its ability to hit a known, previously imaged target with a penetrating warhead, the JASSM does almost the same job as an early F-117. The production price is fixed and is below the Air Force's goal of $400,000.

The Air Force plans to buy 2,400 JASSMs over nine years, at a peak rate of 360 missiles a year. Low-rate initial production should start in 2000, and the missile will become operational first on the B-52, in 2001, followed by the B-1, B-2, and F-16. The B-2 will carry 16 missiles.

The B-2 is likely to carry more weapons as its service career continues. In parallel with JSOW, the Air Force is developing and testing a soft-

A small spoiler is mechanically linked to each weapon bay door. The perforated spoilers deflect airflow that would otherwise be channeled at high speed between the doors, reducing turbulence close to the aircraft.
James C. Goodall

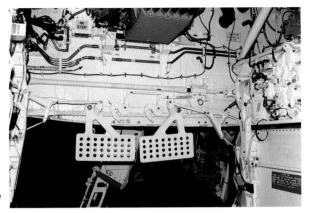

ware package called the Generic Weapons Interface System, which is designed to make it easier to add software for other new guided weapons. Examples include the Lockheed Martin Wind Corrected Munitions Dispenser (WCMD), a tail kit that fits on the standard Tactical Munitions Dispenser. The WCMD tail kit is even simpler than JDAM, because it does not include GPS. The tail kit costs $8,900 (the original estimate was $25,000) and the Air Force plans to acquire 40,000 of them, of which the first 5,000 are earmarked for the Textron Sensor Fused Weapon anti-armour system. The SFW is not yet integrated on the B-2, but it would pose no serious challenges to do so, and it would provide the aircraft with a unique capability.

The SFW was designed to allow a fighter to kill several tanks in one pass. The 1,000-pound dispenser contains 10 BLU-108/B submunitions, each of which carries four drum-shaped sensor-fused warheads or "skeets." The dispenser opens at a predetermined altitude and ejects the submunitions. A parachute slows the submunition and places it in a vertical attitude. Squib rockets fire, lifting and spinning the munition, and the

skeets swing out on mechanical arms and are ejected by centrifugal force.

Each skeet has a narrow-field-of-view infrared sensor. The skeets spin and wobble in flight, so the sensor traces a circular pattern on the ground. When a sensor detects a target, it fires the explosively formed penetrator (EFP) warhead; the charge forges the copper liner of the warhead into a slug, which punches into the target at 5,000 feet/second. The B-2 can carry 36 SFWs on its universal bomb rack—a remarkable total of 1,440 anti-armour munitions on one aircraft—and could drop them in a controlled pattern. Even if each SFW destroys 5 to 10 vehicles (believed to be the design goal), a single pass by a B-2 could disable 180 to 360 vehicles in a column. Air Combat Command documents mention a number of other new B-2 weapons. One of these is the GAM61, a version of the B61-11 with the GAM tail kit. This would allow the B-2 to aim multiple nuclear weapons at the same aimpoint on a single pass. The GAM61 could also be steered into a lofted trajectory after a low-altitude release; to strike the target at the optimum near-vertical angle. A further improvement would be the GAM61-ER (Extended Range), a gliding nuclear weapon with folding wings.

ACC plans also envisage the B-2 carrying a future version of the High-Speed Antiradiation Missile (HARM). The Navy has already funded some test programs aimed at creating a future HARM variant with ramjet propulsion—giving it a range of 100 nautical miles at a speed of Mach 6—and a dual-mode seeker, allowing it to hit enemy radars even if they are turned off while the missile is in flight. This would be an extremely effective defensive weapon for the B-2.

Another way to improve the B-2's ability to suppress air defenses and attack tactical missile

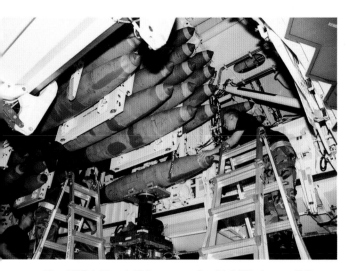

The 509th Bomb Wing crews load Mk82s into a B-2. Each of the B-2's two weapon bays is roughly equal in capacity to the single internal bay on the B-52H. Although the B-52H is a much heavier aircraft, the B-2 has a much larger internal capacity. Even when the B-52 uses external pylons, the B-2 can carry a greater load in some cases, because of its flexible weapon bays. *U.S. Air Force*

A full load of Mk82 500-pound bombs—40 weapons—in just one of the B-2's bomb bays. The full 80-weapon Mk82 load is one of the heaviest carried by the B-2. It would be the weapon load of choice against targets such as ammunition dumps. *U.S. Air Force*

launchers would be to incorporate the Low Cost Autonomous Attack System (LOCAAS). Under development for the USAF by Lockheed Martin, LOCAAS is a small, inexpensive, GPS-guided, jet-powered vehicle with a laser radar (Lidar) and a self-forging projectile warhead like that of the BLU-108. LOCAAS is designed to be launched in groups, each vehicle being programmed to search a given area. The Lidar seeker can identify tanks, missile launchers and SAM systems, and selects the most suitable warhead detonation mode.

LOCAAS is intended to be launched from a captive dispenser on the aircraft. The B-2 could carry 60 of the small weapons in two bays located outboard of the main landing gears.

These are referred to as the "LIB-28" bays, and are currently unused. Their original purpose remains one of the mysteries that surround the B-2, but one Northrop drawing shows them occupied by two cylindrical bodies, resembling pressurized tanks. Whatever the LIB-28 was, it was important enough to rate its own bay and to be provided with frequent-access doors.

The variety of weapons carried by the B-2 indicate that the U.S. Air Force has yet to scratch the surface of its capabilities. Over the next few years, the B-2's operating unit, the 509th Bombardment Wing, will be developing tactics, doctrine, and operational concepts to exploit the unique attributes that have emerged from a long and costly development program.

CHAPTER SIX

THE B-2 IN SERVICE

The 509th Bombardment Wing is dedicated to missions which are of high importance and which only the B-2 can perform. If, for example, the United States decided to destroy a chemical weapons factory in Libya without the B-2, the U.S. government would have to secure landing and overflight permission from one or more NATO allies, either for the attack force (if F-117s were used) or the support force (if B-52s delivered the attack). In either case, the preparations would send a strong signal that an operation was underway. The B-2 can perform the mission, nonstop and unsupported, from Missouri, with one refueling outbound, and can either recover to a U.S. sovereign base such as Diego Garcia in the Indian Ocean or return with another refueling direct to Whiteman.

Training and tactics development are focused on such special, B-2-unique missions. "Gulf War–type operations, where we deploy into a situation and perform like everyone else, are not in the plan now, but we will become deployable," Lieutenant Colonel Jim Whitney of the 394th Combat Training Squadron commented in early 1997.

The 509th is highly selective. Out of 60 to 70 pilots with the necessary paper qualifications to fly the B-2, some 20 are selected for interview. After an interview and a check ride in the Hughes Weapon System Trainer, 7 of these are chosen for B-2 training.

The trainees are midlevel captains with 1,000 hours in bombers or 600 hours in fighters, and ample air-to-air refueling experience. Roughly one-third come from B-1s, one-third from B-52s, and one-third from fighters, mostly F-15s or F-117s. As well as experience and piloting skills, the 509th is looking for people with leadership potential—"People who can be trusted to fly an expensive asset"—and individuals with initiative.

The *Spirit of Missouri* was the first B-2 delivered to the 509th and has now returned to service as a Block 30. Here, the bomber carries the name of its commander for the delivery flight in December 1993: General Mike Loh, commander of Air Combat Command. *U.S. Air Force*

Whiteman Air Force Base in Missouri was modernized with a line of specially built individual shelters for each aircraft. "You don't buy a Lamborghini and park it in the driveway," one Air Force officer explained. Realistically, the Air Force argued that the shelters' built-in fire-suppression systems would cover the entire cost of construction if they saved one aircraft over the life of the B-2. *U.S. Air Force*

Training starts with 178 hours of academics, followed by 60 hours in the cockpit procedures trainer, a fairly basic replica of the B-2 cockpit. The next step is 40 hours of "real time" practice in the mission trainer, another fixed-base system that "teaches pilots to be navigators."

The student then moves on to the Hughes-Link Division Weapon System Trainer (WST), an extremely sophisticated full-motion simulator that doubles as a mission rehearsal system, with access to a global database of targets and threats. Block 20 training required 15 WST flights; the Block 30 takes 19 rides, most of the increase being due to the later version's TF/TA capability. (From the pilot's viewpoint, the Block 10 to Block 20 change has been much more significant than Block 20 to 30.) After 7 WST rides, the pilot takes a first flight in the B-2 and is ready for a check ride by the ninth sortie.

This process, known as initial qualification training, takes six months. After passing the initial qualification training, the pilot typically flies two sorties per month on the B-2, interspersed with four to six flights on the unit's charcoal-gray T-38 companion trainers. Like other specialized U.S. Air Force units, the 509th uses the T-38s to maintain hands-on flying skills and to keep the pilots accustomed to making quick decisions.

The pilot will typically fly for about a year before upgrading to mission commander. The B-2 has a crew of two: the pilot and the mission commander, in the left seat, who combines the roles of the pilot and the weapon system operator and is additionally responsible for targeting and weapon release. As was done on the FB-111, the 509th tries to match pilots and mission commanders according to personality and compatible working methods and to keep crews together over the long term.

Pilots describe the B-2 as a pleasant, undemanding aircraft to fly, a factor that helps to keep the workload reasonable. As in any fly-by-wire aircraft, leaving the stick in the center position means that the aircraft will hold its current attitude. The B-2 is not a fighter: its flying-wing design limits it to a relatively small alpha range, its long wingspan precludes a rapid roll rate, and it does not have the thrust for high-g maneuvering or rapid acceleration. But it is more responsive than most large aircraft, because the control system is powerful and the airframe is stiff. Because of its low drag, it out-accelerates most aircraft of its size, and the fighter-type engines respond quickly to throttle inputs. The verdict, according to one operational pilot: B-52 pilots think the B-2 is maneuverable and B-1 pilots think it is less so. As for

The individual shelters open front and rear so that the B-2's engines can be run up inside the hangar. Fuel and other fluids, and electrical and air services, run in tunnels beneath the floor. Diagnostic hook-ups are also installed. Air-conditioning provides a suitable environment for repairing the bomber's low-observable materials. *U.S. Air Force*

fighter pilots: "It's still a Mack truck to them."

Before the B-2 flew, many critics expected the aircraft to be only marginally stable. Even on the first flight, however, observers noted the B-2's almost unnatural steadiness on final approach, with absolutely no visible wing rock or "hunting" in alpha. The speed brakes are left

Missouri at Palmdale, ready for delivery to the 509th. This view shows the rugged construction of the main landing gear doors and even the auxiliary air inlets: Apertures on a stealth aircraft must be rigid to prevent them from gapping in flight. The weapon bay doors are open and the spoilers are extended. *Northrop*

open 45 degrees up and down on the approach, increasing drag and placing the engines in a more responsive thrust range.

One of the bomber's quirks is apparent on landing: the broad center-body generates a powerful ground cushion, so landings are no-flare, carrier-style affairs, one pilot notes. "If you do try to flare, the airplane says, 'You want to fly, let's go fly.' It's obvious when you see someone do that on one of their first landings." Another pilot observes that "you don't need the flight engineer barking out the radar altitude so that you don't pancake the airplane." On the other hand, the 509th pilots have noticed a tendency toward "firm" landings on the part of pilots making their first T-38 approaches after a series of B-2 flights.

The flight control system normally keeps the B-2 at zero beta (that is to say, with no sideslip or crab) and a constant alpha, selected by the pilot. At low level and high speeds, the constant-alpha law tends to counteract wind gusts immediately: an upward gust increases the aircraft's alpha, and so the FCS commands the aircraft to pitch down. At the same time, the abrupt alpha increase is detected by the gust-alleviation laws in the FCS, which signals the elevons and beavertail to apply more nose-up trim on the outer wings and less on the center-line. This reduces the peak bending moment. The ride quality is not quite as good as that of the B-1 (there is no substitute for very high wing loading) but is much better than a B-52's.

Low-level training was temporarily suspended in early 1997 because of the risk of bird strikes. Crews do not expect the B-2 to be susceptible to catastrophic damage (of the kind that caused the loss of one B-1). Most vital systems are buried deeply behind the leading edges and front spars, and even the largest bird will have been slowed down by a few authoritative ricochets before it can reach the engines. The B-2 force cannot afford to have an aircraft down for extensive repairs, however, because it would disrupt the training schedule.

The entire B-2 in-flight refueling envelope was cleared in a single flight, a first-time achievement for a brand-new aircraft. This is not to say that refueling is always easy. The KC-10 is not much of a problem, with its size and a very long boom, but the KC-135 represents a unique situation. The B-2's refueling slipway is located well aft, and unlike most conventional aircraft, is behind much of the wing. The entire aircraft must be driven through two "downbursts"—one off the engines and one off

As the 509th received more aircraft, it became more common to see more than one B-2 in the air at once. Here, *South Carolina*—in Block 10 configuration—is prepared for a training flight as another B-2 takes to the air. *Northrop*

the wing—to reach a contact position. Once the B-2 is in position, it is well inside the KC-135's "bubble" and the two aircraft interact strongly: any movement of one aircraft tends to affect the other. "Once you're inside the tanker's envelope, the B-2 tends to slide forward on you because you're so clean."

But flying the B-2 is a great deal more than stick-and-rudder skills, because of the bomber's complex systems. "If an individual likes computer games, it suits them very well," says one pilot. "You can fly for a long time and never touch the stick or throttles. The automation frees up a lot of brain power for other tasks." The challenge is teaching the pilot where to find the information needed to accomplish the mission.

Pilots who grew up with computer games sometimes forget that the B-2 was designed in the early 1980s. One pilot calls this the "shock,

Washington, in Block 10 configuration, on a training flight. Clearly visible here is the B-2's extensive "antenna farm," above the avionics bays in the central hummock. The antennas—seen as diamond-shaped patches—are specially designed, located in RAM-treated cavities, and covered with panels which permit only specified frequencies to pass through. *Northrop*

denial, and acceptance" syndrome: "When you start, you're always behind the system. Once you've trained, you can be waiting for the system and saying, 'Come on, I'm burning nanoseconds here.'"

A GATS/GAM attack is one of the most difficult tasks on the B-2. The pilot has to fly an indirect path to the target, while the mission commander searches for the target and a secondary reference point on the SAR scope. F-15E and B-1 people find it easy, apparently, but others find radar signal interpretation difficult. The APQ-181 is good, but performance does vary with obscurants and the size of the targets. "We start with big buildings in the middle of nowhere and move on to more difficult targets," one pilot comments. GATS/GAM is "not a problem with the processors on the airplane, but with the gray matter in the pilot's head."

One unique aspect of the 509th's operations, directly related to its "sniper squadron" role, is that some of its missions may be extremely long. The worst case is a nonstop mission halfway around the world and back, using an indirect route to avoid violating airspace. So far the longest real mission flown by a B-2 has been a 37-hour, 14,414-nautical mile flight from Whiteman to Guam and back, and crews have flown mission rehearsals for up to 44.5 hours in the Weapon System Trainer.

The simulations are as realistic as the WST can make them, including equipment failures and threats, and if the real mission will start at 2 A.M., the simulation does so as well. Pilots have experimented with different kinds of bedding and food; the B-2 cockpit is just large enough for a roll-up mattress and can accommodate a chemical toilet and a few personal items. Crews on the simulator rides are heavily instrumented, including an eye-blink-rate sensor attached to the oxygen mask, and their performance in air-to-air refueling and weapon delivery is carefully monitored. So far, tests have shown that a combination of preflight rest and "power napping" during the tedious parts of the flight should make it possible to fly missions of more than 50 hours without degrading the crew's performance over the target.

Whiteman was identified as the first base for the B-2 in 1986; it had not hosted large aircraft since the 1960s, when a B-47 wing gave way to Minuteman missiles. The base was largely rebuilt to accommodate the new aircraft, including a row of individual docks for each bomber. Each dock opens at both ends (so that engines can be started under cover), has underfloor plumbing for fuel and fluids, and includes comprehensive test equipment and a fire-suppression system.

The B-2 maintenance crews typically compare themselves to the "Maytag repairman," referring to the long-running advertising campaign for Maytag washers, featuring the repairman whose phone never rings. The B-2 does require a fair amount of scheduled maintenance because of its complexity, but it seldom breaks—a result of the rigorous specifications, long development, and meticulous testing.

The main area where maintenance lessons are still being learned concerns stealth. Like

The 2,000-pound Boeing GBU-31 Joint Direct Attack Munition (JDAM) is the B-2's primary conventional weapon. The JDAM kit comprises a self-contained tail unit and a "jacket" carrying four stabilizing fins. The guidance system consists of a low-cost inertial/GPS unit and movable tailfins and steers the bomb to follow the path predicted by the bomber's weapon-aiming software. *James C. Goodall*

B-2s of the 509th Bombardment Wing prepare for a training mission. During 1998, the wing demonstrated its ability to deploy multiple aircraft on a single mission and to send aircraft for extended deployments overseas. *U.S. Air Force*

A B-2 lifts off from Andersen Air Force Base, Guam, during the bomber's first extended overseas deployment in March 1998. Operating from three bases—Whiteman, Andersen, and Diego Garcia—B-2s can reach almost any likely target on the globe with a single in-flight refueling. *U.S. Air Force*

the F-117, the B-2 is requiring excessive low observable (LO) maintenance in its early years and is undergoing a series of modifications intended to reduce the maintenance burden.

F-117 experience was not very helpful to the B-2 program for two main reasons: the B-2 was being designed while the F-117 was just entering service, and the B-2 uses a different approach to stealth design. As noted earlier, the aircraft used shaping rather than a heavy coat of RAM to achieve stealth, but one consequence of the aircraft's design was that small discontinuities and gaps could create very significant "hot-spots" on the skin. In a large aircraft, too, significant flexing and bending is unavoidable and causes each skin panel to

move relative to its neighbors in ways that are virtually impossible to predict.

While the B-2 represented a technological advance over the F-117 in terms of combining LO with aerodynamic efficiency, it was similar in that LO was given higher priority than maintainability. The B-2 was designed for nuclear strike, so the force would be divided at any time between alert aircraft—in full LO trim, but not flying—and aircraft on training missions. It did not matter too much if the LO treatment would need extensive work after one or two sorties, because the alert aircraft would not fly more than two sorties.

Most of the B-2 surface has not been a problem, according to Colonel William Armstrong,

The 21st and last B-2, *Spirit of Louisiana*, climbs away from Andersen during the March 1998 deployment. *Louisiana* was one of two B-2s delivered in Block 30 configuration. The bomber's main landing gear units retract forward, behind vault-like one-piece doors. *U.S. Air Force*

Spirit of Washington climbs into a gray Missouri sky. The exhausts are larger than they appear here: From the rear, the exit nozzle is masked by the aft decks. These have posed a complex structural challenge, and the original deck design has been replaced. *Bill Sweetman*

AV-20, *Pennsylvania*, slides up to a KC-135 on the way to the March 1998 Guam deployment. The visual distinguishing mark of the Block 30 is the seamless leading edge, installed to rectify the RCS problems that were discovered in 1991. Regardless of block number, however, all B-2s seen from this angle appear to have crew clipboards resting on the 40-acre cockpit coaming. *U.S. Air Force*

chief of the fighter/bomber maintenance division at Air Combat Command headquarters; however, some of the original materials used to seal joints and gaps were selected for their LO performance with little attention to other qualities. Some of them, particularly the caulk and tape materials used to fill joint lines and seal access panels, "were toxic or hazardous," says Armstrong. "They had short lives and long cure times, measured in days or weeks."

Sealants were subject to cracking, peeling, and loss of adhesion caused by air loads, rain, and structural distortion. Some materials were applied in as many as five layers "and if the fourth layer did not cure properly, you had to remove everything and start from scratch." In other cases, long seams had to be filled in sections, with substantial cure times between each section. One caulking material would take 35 days to cure at normal temperatures. It would cure in 72 hours if heated, but only 3 feet of caulk could be cured at a time. Many of the materials would not cure properly outside a controlled environment, avoiding extremes of temperature or humidity.

Early B-2 maintenance horror stories, inspired by a 1997 report from Congress' General Accounting Office (GAO), were primarily based on service experience with the Block 10 and Block 20. The Block 30 variant is a great improvement, featuring "a tremendous evolutionary change in materials," according to Armstrong. As noted earlier, all the edges and coatings are removed and replaced, but some of the most awkward materials have been almost completely eliminated. The Block 10/20 used "several thousand feet" of the 72-hour, heat-cured caulk mentioned above to seal panel lines. On the Block 30, only 60 feet of the material is left, most of it replaced by a new thin-tape material. Cure times on other materials have been reduced "from days to hours," says Armstrong.

The GAO's mid-1998 report, notes that, in themselves, the Block 30 changes will not allow the B-2 to achieve the 77 percent mission capable rate. This is correct, says Armstrong, but the mission capable rate is limited by a number of factors, of which maintenance of the LO system is one. The Air Force is planning to invest in improvements to bring the B-2 up to its specified reliability in the early 2000s.

LO maintenance accounts for 40 percent of the unscheduled maintenance on the B-2, and 31 percent of its total maintenance. Currently, with the Block 20 in the process of being superseded by the Block 30 as the principal operational variants, the fleet is running between 70 and 100 maintenance man hours per flight

A B-2 approaches a KC-135 over Missouri. Whiteman Air Force Base is visible under the bomber's wingtip, at right. The longest B-2 mission so far, at 37.6 hours, involved five in-flight refuelings and covered 15,000 miles. *U.S. Air Force*

A B-2 floats in for landing. The B-2 is a naturally slippery aircraft and wants to gain speed in a descent, so the brake-rudders are kept open to increase drag and stabilize the aircraft with the engines at a reasonable power setting. In the event of a go-around, the brakes can be closed rapidly and the airplane will pull up quickly. *Northrop*

hour (MMH/FH). The Air Force's goal for the B-2 was 50 MMH/FH. Recently, Congress has authorized the release of $54 million in FY 1998 money to start a set of initiatives that, Armstrong believes, will put the B-2 MMH/FH "in the low- to mid-40s."

It should be noted, at this point, that a 50 MMH/FH figure for the B-2 is quite attractive to the operator, given that the bomber's offensive war load is eight to ten times larger than that of the average fighter. A fighter would have to achieve 5 to 6 MMH/FH to put as many weapons on target for the same maintenance burden.

Several main improvements are planned. One is the use of "alternate high-frequency

The B-2 makes rare air-show appearances and is even more seldom seen on the ground away from an operational base. *Nebraska* was part of the static display at the Air Force's 50th anniversary show at Nellis Air Force Base in Nevada in April 1997, carrying the names of Air Force Chief of Staff General Ron Fogelman and Air Combat Command leader General Richard Hawley. *Bill Sweetman*

materials" for access panels that are used often. Some access panels on the B-2, which are opened as often as once per mission, must be caulked or taped and then covered with a top coat to preserve the integrity of the LO system. The Air Force plans to coat the panels and surrounding areas with a new magnetic-type RAM (that is, one in which the absorber is magnetic rather than dielectric), which is tolerant of small gaps, eliminating the need to seal the panels.

The new HF material will also be used around drain ports in the lower surface. The B-2 was designed with "push-drain" apertures that are closed in flight, to maintain stealth, and can be opened on the ground to release water and other fluids. However, the pooling and freezing of water inside the aircraft has caused problems. With the new material, drain holes can be left open.

The B-2 will receive an advanced top coat, the paint-like coating that covers most of the surface. It will be more flexible than today's topcoat material, which has tended to crack at stress points and will be more durable, lasting for 10 years before it is removed and replaced. Finally, like the F-117, the B-2 will make use of new heat-resistant tiles in the exhaust area. Overall, the Air Force aims to reduce the number of different types of materials on the B-2, particularly those that are difficult to apply, hazardous to handle, and that have a limited shelf life.

The U.S. Air Force plans to flight-test these improvements on AV-3 in 2000, as the last Block 30s are delivered, and to incorporate them as the B-2s return to the factory for scheduled depot maintenance. The exception is one access panel at the junction of the engine-bay and tailpipe access doors, which is apparently troublesome and

will be recoated with the new HF magnetic RAM before the rest of the aircraft.

One important deficiency has affected all stealth aircraft, until recently: there was no way to measure the RCS of an aircraft in service. The only way to ensure that an aircraft was stealthy, before it was launched on a mission, was to ensure that there were no detectable blemishes on its external surfaces. Since a physically small defect can cause a dangerous reflection, this required painstaking inspection and frequent small repairs.

To solve this problem, the technology developed to test RCS models in indoor and outdoor test ranges is being adapted for production and flight-line use. Northrop Grumman has acquired three Systems Planning Corporation Mk V radar systems to perform "production point inspection" on the Block 30s as they leave the assembly line. "Now, when we build a B-2 and take it to the range and test it, it passes on the first try," according to Military Aircraft Systems Division vice-president Bill Lawler. The Air Force is making some use of these radars. The contractor has also developed a hand-held point inspection device, which is being used by its personnel working at Whiteman Air Force Base.

When a B-2 is on static display, the public is kept at a respectful distance. Details of the exhaust system remain sensitive, so the aircraft is usually parked nose-on to the crowd and is not moved until the show is over for the day. *Bill Sweetman*

117

Designed primarily to remain undetected by radars below it, the B-2 has a smooth, featureless underside. Even at this angle, the inlets are completely masked by the wing and only the top of the windshield is visible. *Bill Sweetman*

These devices are a precursor to a program called Common LO Verification Systems (CLOVRS), which includes point tools and "near-field" inspection tools. One example of the latter is DIRS (Diagnostic Imaging Radar System), which has been acquired to support the F-117. Developed by Systems Planning Corporation, DIRS includes a special radar system mounted on a portable track that encircles the aircraft, allowing it to view the aircraft from all relevant angles. A similar system will be incorporated in the definitive CLOVRS system, which could be delivered as early as 2000 to 2001.

Some LO restoration materials will continue to demand an environment with controlled humidity and temperature. The Air Force is acquiring an operational prototype of a transportable, air-conditioned hangar for the B-2. If it is successful, the Air Force will acquire more of them and position them at likely forward operating locations.

Some LO maintenance lessons emerged when two B-2 Block 30 aircraft were deployed to Andersen Air Force Base, Guam, in March and April 1998—the bomber's first large-scale deployment overseas. One was a need to reduce the bomber's logistics "footprint" (the two bombers did not pack light for the trip, being

The B-2's unique "beak" nose is a result of a compromise between the aerodynamicists and the electromagnetics wizards. The sharp edge, required for stealth performance, is angled downward to meet the relative airflow around the B-2's forward fuselage. *Bill Sweetman*

attended by 170 tons of equipment and 197 people). The same concern applies to expeditionary use of the B-1 and B-52 and could be alleviated by better planning, leaner staffing, and pre-positioning of heavy equipment.

The exercise "did not look at full LO maintenance," says Armstrong. Rather, the Air Force was interested in how well the LO systems would survive without major restoration work, and the aircraft were tested before they were deployed and after they returned. Some LO restoration was done in the open air, and "some

A B-2 makes a night takeoff. The high-intensity lights on the main landing gear legs are illuminating the doors and bays, and the wingtip-mounted retractable navigation lights are also visible. *U.S. Air Force*

Neither the B-52H nor the B-1B looks like anything else in the sky, but both look positively conventional beside the B-2. Because there are so few B-2s, Air Combat Command is developing concepts of operations that exploit the bombers' different characteristics and weapons. *U.S. Air Force*

This is included for the benefit of the reporter who asked the author: "Is the stealth fighter designed to escort the stealth bomber?" Two contrasts are apparent here: the faceted shape of the F-117, beside the seamless B-2, and the fact that the B-2 is seven times the weight of the F-117 and carries ten times as much over five times the distance, but measures only 4 feet longer from nose to tail. *U.S. Air Force*

of the materials liked the climate," according to Armstrong. Overall, "we did not see a lot of degradation," he says. A significant discovery was that "we don't have to be as intensive in the way we restore the aircraft. Small defects can be allowed to accumulate, and they don't have a big signature effect." On the other hand, lacking flight-line LO diagnostic tools, "we don't know how far we can allow it to go."

In the long term, it has been suggested, flight-line diagnostic systems could generate a map of LO hot-spots that could be read by the mission-planning system. Currently, LO mission planners assume that the aircraft is maintained to its design specifications, but this may not be necessary, depending on the location of the target and the nature of the threat. The Air Force's Common LO Auto-Router could interface with CLOVRS so that the crew would be able to plan routes that would mask deficiencies from the most dangerous threats.

As these words are written, in late 1998, the B-2 is expected to become fully operational by late 1999. The 509th is continuing to practice forward deployments, of the kind that would show U.S. resolve to use force in future crises. In late September 1998, three B-2s deployed to Andersen Air Force Base on Guam, together with three B-52H bombers from Barksdale Air Force Base. The bombers constituted the 2nd Air Expeditionary Group, a provisional unit formed to exploit the unique capabilities of the newest and oldest Air Force combat aircraft. During the deployment, the 2nd AEG flew 34 training missions, ranging as far north as South Korea and as far east as Wake Island.

Joint bomber operations form part of the U.S. Air Force's fast-paced program to form its combat aircraft into 10 Air Expeditionary Force (AEF) groups. The AEF concept involves assigning U.S. Air Force combat and support aircraft into 10 175-aircraft groups, including fighters, bombers, tankers, transports, and rescue aircraft. The AEFs will be numbered and named (two have been named after Generals Arnold and Mitchell, two of the founders of U.S. military aviation). Flight and maintenance crews will be assigned permanently to an AEF and will wear its insignia. The AEFs will train, deploy, and regroup on a two-year cycle. The system is loosely patterned on the U.S. Navy's organization of carrier air groups.

Most of the time, however, Air Force aircraft and crews will be based and supported as they are today, in the existing structure of bases, wings, and squadrons. Only two AEFs will be deployed at any time, while two more will be training in preparation for deployment.

Bombers will be an essential element of the AEF, because they can be over their targets more rapidly than fighters. In a crisis, the bombers can be over their targets within 24 hours of a decision to go, while fighters are still on their way to their forward bases. There are not enough B-2s to cover all 10 AEFs—at most, the AEF will have three B-2s on strength, backed up by B-1Bs or B-52s—and this is why the 509th is training jointly with B-52s. The B-2 can penetrate air defenses and deliver heavy loads of guided bombs; the B-52 carries conventional long-range cruise missiles and highly accurate AGM-142 stand-off missiles today and will carry the AGM-158 JASSM in the near future. Between them, a small force of these heavy bombers can damage a large number and wide variety of targets in a single mission.

In the New World Disorder of the 21st century, the B-2 has found a mission. What it does not have, as yet, is a name. In accordance with U.S. Air Force tradition, the official name "Spirit" is never heard around the aircraft. The name "Bat" has been suggested (it fits neatly with the one-syllable Buff and Bone) but has not caught on. Neither has Voron, Russian for raven and the call-sign for B-2 flight tests. The less respectful "Porkchop" has been quoted in some places, and

The B-2 will remain in service until 2040, if it matches the longevity of the B-52H.

anyone who has seen a B-2 turning at a distance will recognize its origin. Meanwhile, crews call it simply "the jet" and there is no doubt at Whiteman as to what that means.

The B-2 is an extremely complex and technologically advanced aircraft that has emerged from a long, controversial development program. It has suffered, and still suffers, from being at the mercy of decisions made by people who do not understand its capabilities.

Myths and misconceptions about the B-2 are everywhere and will be destroyed only gradually. As Mark Twain remarked, "A lie can be halfway around the world before the truth has got its boots on."

The B-2's builders and operators are confident that the fully operational aircraft will be stealthy enough to perform its mission: to deliver 16 near-precision, hard-target weapons per sortie, anywhere in the world, with no support except tankers. There is nothing else in the world that even comes close to this capability, nor will there be for decades. The B-2's capabilities will be unique when most of us have retired.

It still seems puzzling and incongruous that, while there is no money for more B-2s, the Pentagon is pushing hard for a Joint Strike Fighter that will not be much more survivable than a B-2, at best; carries one-eighth of its weapon load; has one-fifth of its unrefueled range; relies on the availability of overseas bases; and will not be available for another decade. Are numbers everything?

More than half a century ago, the U.S. Army Air Corps wanted to buy a new bomber. It was large, sophisticated, and the most expensive combat aircraft in the world.

Critics in Congress and the other branches of the military argued that economic times were tight and that the United States was not about to become embroiled in any conflicts where the big bomber's unique assets—range and survivability—would be necessary. A cheaper warplane, based on an existing airframe to save money, would be adequate.

The Air Corps lost its fight and received only a small test squadron of the big bombers. Most of the money earmarked for bombers went to buy hundreds of the less expensive aircraft.

The cheaper bomber was the Douglas B-18A Bolo, a derivative of the DC-2 airliner. In the Air Force Museum in Dayton, Ohio, a plaque in front of an immaculate B-18 sums up its front-line combat career: "Several of these aircraft were destroyed by the Japanese on December 7, 1941."

The big, costly bomber that the nation could not afford was, of course, the Boeing B-17 Flying Fortress.

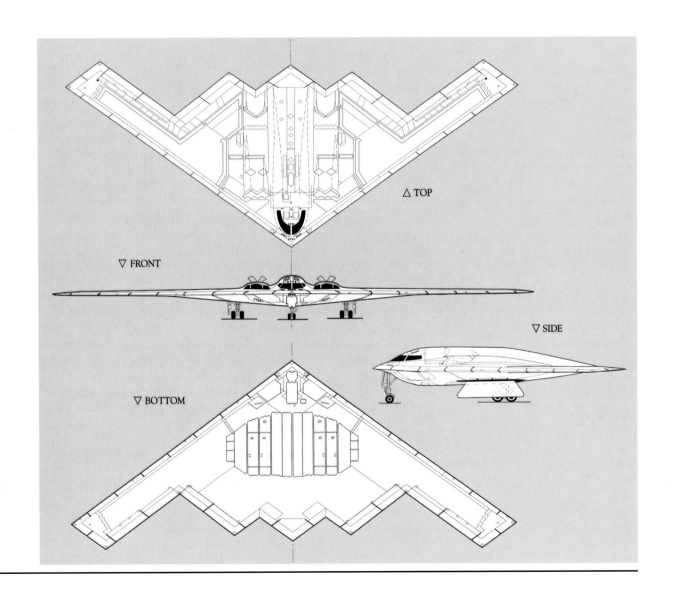

△ TOP

▽ FRONT

▽ SIDE

▽ BOTTOM

124

B-2 DATA

Dimensions

Wingspan   172 feet (52.4 meters)
Length   69 feet (21 meters)
Wing area   5,140 feet^2 (477.5 meters^2)

Propulsion

4 x GE F118-GE-100, 19,000-pound thrust (84.5 kN) each

Weights

Operational empty   153,700 pounds (69,705 kilograms)
Fuel capacity   180,000 pounds (81,635 kilograms)
Max weapon load   50,000 pounds (22,700 kilograms)
Normal takeoff   336,500 pounds (152,607 kilograms)

Performance

Cruising speed   Mach 0.85/485 kt/900 kilometers per hour at 36,000 feet
Speed at sea level   Mach 0.8/530 kt/980 kilometers per hour
Service ceiling   Above 50,000 feet

Range, Unrefueled

Weapons	Weight (Pounds, approximate)	Low-altitude Segment (Nautical Miles)	Unrefueled Range (Nautical Miles)
16 JDAM	37,000	1,000	4,410
16 JDAM	37,000	0	6,300

PRODUCTION AND DELIVERIES
Development

Air Vehicle	Serial	First Flight	Name	Delivered as Block 30
1001 (AV-1)	82-1066	July 17, 1989		6/00
1002 (AV-2)	82-1067	Oct. 19, 1990	*Arizona*	3/98
1003 (AV-3)*	82-1068	June 18, 1991	*New York*	6/00
1004 (AV-4)	82-1069	April 17, 1992		5/99
1005 (AV-5)	82-1070	Oct. 5, 1992	*Ohio*	1/00
1006 (AV-6)	82-1071	Feb. 2, 1993	*Mississippi*	5/98

Production

Air Vehicle	Serial	Name	Delivered	Block	Upgraded/Delivered Block 20	Block 30
1007	88-0328	*Texas*	8/94	10		9/98
1008	88-0329	*Missouri*	12/93	10		11/97
1009	88-0330	*California*	8/94	10		6/98
1010	88-0331	*South Carolina*	12/94	10		4/98
1011	88-0332	*Washington*	10/94	10		12/98
1012	89-0127	*Kansas*	2/95	10	9/96	3/99
1013	89-0128	*Nebraska*	9/95	10	7/96	7/99
1014	89-0129	*Georgia*	11/95	10	5/97	9/99
1015	90-0040	*Alaska*	1/96	10	3/97	4/00
1016	90-0041	*Hawaii*	12/95	10	11/96	5/00
1017	92-0700	*Florida*	7/96	20		12/99
1018	93-1085	*Oklahoma*	5/96	20		7/00
1019	93-1086	*Kitty Hawk*	8/96	20		2/00
1020	93-1087	*Pennsylvania*	8/97	30		
1021	93-1088	*Louisiana*	12/97	30		

DEFENSE CONSOLIDATION AND THE B-2 TEAM

Current Team Member	Original Team Member	Responsibility
Northrop Grumman	Northrop	Prime contractor, integrator, forward fuselage, edges and LO systems
Northrop Grumman	Vought	Intermediate fuselage structures
Boeing		Outer wings, center fuselage, landing gear, rotary weapon launchers
Boeing	McDonnell Douglas	Airframe components
Boeing	Rockwell North American	Airframe components
General Electric		F118 engines
Raytheon Systems	Hughes	APQ-181 radar
Raytheon Systems	Link	Weapon system trainers
Raytheon Systems	Raytheon	EW system components
Lockheed Martin	General Electric	Flight control system
Lockheed Martin	IBM Federal Systems	APR-50 Defensive Management System
Lockheed Martin	Unisys	Mission computers
AlliedSignal		APU
Rockwell Collins		Communications equipment
Orbital Sciences	Fairchild	Data storage system
Rosemount		Air data system

Note: These changes result from the 1993–1998 consolidation of the defense industry.

INDEX